PHILANTHROPY: THE CITY STORY

'IN FAITH AND HOPE THE WORLD WILL DISAGREE BUT ALL MANKIND'S CONCERN IS CHARITY'

Alexander Pope, 1734

First published 2013, by Sutton's Hospital, Charterhouse Square, London, EC1M 6AN

Published to accompany the exhibition *Philanthropy: the City Story*, held at the Charterhouse, 29 October – 30 November, 2013. The idea originated from Dominic Tickell and has been realised through the partnership between the Charterhouse and the Museum of London. Both partners are grateful to the City of London Corporation's charity City Bridge Trust for generous support. They would like to thank the project's steering group: Hilary Browne-Wilkinson, Jenny Field, Richard Foley, Bill Frazer, Perdita Hunt, Menna McGregor, Ainslie Ross, Jane Ruddell, Clare Thomas and Wilf Weeks: with special thanks to steering-group member Cheryl Chapman for her contribution.

A CIP catalogue record for this publication is available from the British Library.

ISBN 978-0-9927109-0-3

Designed by Joe Ewart for Society

Principal photography by Lawrence Watson
www.lawrencewatsonphotography.com

Cover motif designed by Jayne Davies

City of London map:
www.janeillustration.co.uk

Printed by Press to Print Ltd

PICTURE CREDITS

Sutton's Hospital: p. 23 (left).

City of London Corporation: pp. 6, 59, 68, 70.

Joe Ewart: p. 23 (right).

The Mercers' Company/photographer Louis Sinclair: pp. 18, 22 (left), 24 (right).

Museum of London: front cover (1 portrait); pp. 9, 12 (right), 14, 15 (right), 19–21, 27, 28, 30, 31–34, 36 (right), 38, 39 (left), 41, 42 (right), 43 (right), 44–47.

National Portrait Gallery: front cover (3 portraits); pp. 29, 39 (right).

Lawrence Watson: pp. 4, 6, 8, 10, 11, 12 (left), 13, 15 (left), 16/17, 22 (right), 24 (left), 25, 26, 35, 36 (left), 37, 40, 42 (left), 43 (right), 48/49, 51, 52, 53, 57/58, 64, 80.

Cover flaps: (detail)
*London from Southwark, c.*1630.
The painting was given to Whitechapel Library in 1892 by the philanthropist Sir Samuel Montagu. It was subsequently acquired by the Museum of London.
© Museum of London.

CONTENTS

FOREWORD

This book is an exploration of the history of philanthropy in the Square Mile. So much of the City – bridges, hospitals, schools, sanitation, almshouses and churches – was brought into creation thanks to our forebears, including our most famous Lord Mayor, Dick Whittington.

The word 'philanthropy' is taken from the Greek 'for the love of humanity'. From medieval to modern times, the City's livery companies, civic leaders and businesses have assumed a responsibility for meeting public need. They understood the importance of investing in their communities and the necessity of being a part of, not apart from, society.

This book tells the story of the far-sighted people who made and gave away incredible fortunes – laying firm foundations for the City and the Nation. In meeting the pressing necessities of life for the Londoners of their day, and before income taxes were levied to meet social need, philanthropy was certainly a moral choice – but it was something more besides. Those people also perceived long-term investment in the community to be in their own best interests; a well-looked-after society is a contented society, and one that works better and more peacefully than one that isn't.

This is 'enlightened self-interest' – a philosophy practised by Andrew Carnegie, the Scottish-American industrialist who led the expansion of the steel industry in the 19th Century and was possibly one of history's greatest philanthropists. He gave $350 million to charity before his death in 1919 – impelled by his own "Carnegie Dictum" to spend the first third of one's life getting all the education one can, spend the next third making all the money one can and spend the last third giving it all away to worthwhile causes.

The City of London's success is built on a long-term investment in community – the two are interdependent. Social need is all around us and it is in our interests to meet that need. And nowadays, it's not just in addressing material poverty but also poverty of the mind.

This book highlights the important relationship between philanthropy and business – operating together to drive development and support our society. In addition, centuries of philanthropic practice and an understanding of the value of endowed capital has ensured the UK has well-established and effective charity and tax laws – making London a global centre for managing international philanthropic funds.

We want to reinvigorate the City's role as an engine of philanthropy for the UK – engaging a new generation of dynamic, entrepreneurial business leaders to make their own investment decisions where they perceive a need. New models of giving through micro-finance, social investment and venture philanthropy can afford excellent opportunities for the City to apply its creativity and capital to maximise the impact of the third sector.

Many new networks, organisations and initiatives are being launched to encourage and expand philanthropy. The City of London Corporation's charity, City Bridge Trust, is committed to engaging professionals at the very start of their careers – embedding philanthropic giving in their thinking. The Museums Association has found that, at present, only 7% of people in the UK leave money to any charity when they die. In contrast, the UK's greatest and oldest philanthropic group – the livery companies of the City of London – have recently reaffirmed a long-standing tradition of giving with the Livery Legacy Initiative. New liverymen and women are asked to make a commitment in favour of their livery company's charitable interests from their eventual estate which, with current inheritance tax breaks for charitable donations, makes good sense.

This book, and the exhibition it accompanies, will explore the contribution and motivation of some great City philanthropists – acting on 'enlightened self-interest' and continuing to build strong, successful societies.

I encourage you to contemplate and celebrate *Philanthropy: The City Story*.

Alderman Roger Gifford
The Rt. Hon. the Lord Mayor of London

1 | Leadenhall Market. The market was originally built for public use as a granary by Alderman Simon Eyre in 1346.

PHILANTHROPY: THE CITY'S PAST

CHARITY AND CITY

I am now come to the strength and power of this city, which consisteth partly in the number of the citizens themselves
  John Stow, 1603

London is one of the world's most successful cities. It is a famously dynamic and entrepreneurial place, and has been so for centuries. 'Rich, busy, hurrying London' wrote the German Professor Frederick von Raumer in 1836, '... always the sharp outline of reality; the mathematics of life; the arts of calculating, of gaining, of governing'. This was a place of practical action. The roles of business and government as channels for the entrepreneurial energies of London's citizens are well known. But this book, and the exhibition that it accompanies, explores philanthropy as an alternative catalyst of enterprise and achievement over the centuries.

The focus is on philanthropy in the City of London, a place where London's spirit of enterprise is distilled to the maximum. The City is the historic core of London and also, arguably, the historic centre of charitable-giving in Britain. It was in the City that many forms of charitable activity originated or evolved into business models for others to follow. The City has been the place where many heated debates about philanthropy have aired. Today, philanthropy is often couched in terms of fairness, of 'giving something back'. But the City's history reveals a far more entrepreneurial

2 | Silver Alms Dish, from St Michael's Church, Crooked Lane, hallmark for 1524.
Inscribed 'THIS IS SAYNT MIHEILS BASSON FOR THE EWSE OF THE PORRE, 1564'.
Courtesy St. Magnus the Martyr, London Bridge.

side. For many centuries philanthropy and business in the City have been two sides of the same coin, both experimenting with new ways of using money and ideas to make things happen. And as with business, philanthropy has brought into being organisations that have stood the test of time: alongside its fair share of failed schemes built on wishful-thinking or folly.

Today, the City's legacy of philanthropic activity is visible well beyond the boundaries of the Square Mile. Peabody housing estates, Waterlow Park, the Geffrye Museum, Goldsmiths College and Wimbledon Common are among the many places in London that owe their current character, in part, to City-based philanthropists. Further afield, there are countless schools and academies, parks, bridges, almshouses, universities and charities with links back to London. Within today's City the legacy is less visible. Most of the major charitable institutions have moved out. There are no historic almshouses left within the City boundaries (although the Charterhouse lies just beyond), and only four endowed schools, from a former roll-call of over 20. The one exception to the exodus of major institutions is St Bartholomew's Hospital, which still operates from the same spot on which it was founded in 1123; and where for many centuries it was run by the City and 'endowed by the citizens' benevolence', as John Stow put it in 1603.

Despite the institutional exodus, a few clues to the City's philanthropic past remain visible in today's landscape of offices and busy streets. A scattering of blue plaques mark sites of philanthropic relevance: the statue of George Peabody stands outside the Royal Exchange; and several monuments can still be seen within the City's churches, reciting the benevolence of London's former citizens. Ten charity children statues survive in the City; admittedly this total includes the two on display in the Museum of London's galleries, but they are genuine City children, formerly standing over the door of the Castle Baynard ward school at 6, Sermon Lane.

The modest nature of the physical remains should not be taken as evidence that the City as a place is any less philanthropically-minded today than it was in the past.

3 | Statue of George Peabody by W.W. Story, Royal Exchange Buildings, 1869.

Rather, it underlines the point that philanthropy in the City, like business, is constantly evolving into new forms. One of the great City events of the past was the annual meeting of the charity school children at St Paul's Cathedral [fig 27]: today it is the Lord Mayor's Show, where eye-catching floats underline that the City's livery companies are more charitably-active than ever. For the Square Mile's working population, philanthropy is part of the modern business world. Wealth, corporate social responsibility and personal ethics are all subjects of conversation and debate. Giving is noted in newspapers and donors are ranked on websites. Some speculate about London entering a 'new golden age' of philanthropy.

The resurgence of interest in philanthropy has also touched historians, who are asking new questions about this aspect of Britain's past, bringing new evidence to light and suggesting new ways of understanding what it all means. This, then, seems a good time to reflect on the City's philanthropic past, albeit only in a short overview of a subject that cries out for a far longer and more detailed treatment.

If charity is less visible in today's City, that was certainly not the case in former times. The City's history teems with evidence of charitable activity being given prominence and public praise. From the Tudor merchant Robert Dow, whose funerary monument praises the £3,528 he gave for 'diverse charitable deeds' during his lifetime [fig. 6]; to the early-nineteenth-century practice of publishing the names of those who subscribed to appeals for relieving distress in Spitalfields. In 1816 the lists printed in *The Times* included 'three children in Cheapside' who gave £9.

What was it about the City that created what might be called its philanthropic DNA, something that pushed or pulled its citizens towards a habit of benevolence? Speculation might pick out four strands in the City's character. Most obviously, there is the simple presence of wealth, a characteristic that has been pretty constant throughout the ages. 'Charity' as Betsy Rogers has remarked, 'was born of the marriage of Poverty with Abundance', and the City has always had no difficulty in fulfilling the abundance side of the formula.

4 | *(left)* North Gate of St Bartholomew's Hospital, rebuilt 1702-3: the statue of King Henry VIII is by Francis Bird.

5 | *(above)* Blue plaque in Newgate Street.

Less obviously perhaps, at least from today's point of view, is the presence of poverty; but this is also one of the City's characteristics. For centuries the City was the only urban settlement in the region, and an extraordinarily large one at that. All today's familiar urban challenges – sanitation, care for the sick, prisoners' welfare, education of the young, homelessness, vagrancy and more – presented themselves in the medieval City. Much early charitable action, although framed in pious language, must also have been a practical response to these very visible and no doubt distressing conditions. As John Stow implied in 1603, London's exceptional charitable activity stemmed in part from the size of London's problems:

> [London] relieves plentifully and with good policy, not only her own poor people, a thing which scarcely any other town or shire does, but also the poor that from each quarter of the realm do flock unto it.

Poverty remained familiar in the City right up to the nineteenth century, thanks in no small part to the proximity of Spitalfields. This was the City's most familiar urban black-spot, a place where an entire group of artisans had fallen into poverty, seemingly through no fault of their own. The starving handloom-weavers of Spitalfields were a terrible reminder of the failure of local welfare systems and the possible failure of the national mission. Charitable initiatives focussed on Spitalfields from the eighteenth century onwards were legion, including a whole typology of soup kitchens: from Huguenot charities, through Alexis Soyer's model soup kitchen to the soup kitchen for the Jewish poor, first opened in 1854.

The third thread in the City's philanthropic DNA is charity. Charity is, of course, a religious virtue but also a secular one. It offers a way of visualising the links between rich and poor for both believers and non-believers. It is a virtue that demands practical action and thus suits the City of London well. The link with religious belief cannot be underplayed, given the importance of religion in the City's past, both public and private. The dominant value-system in the Square Mile has passed through several religious phases over the centuries: from pious Catholic City through ostentatiously Protestant City to its pragmatic modern phase as a City with a built-in

6 | *(far left)* Robert Dow's monument in St Botolph Aldgate. Dow died in 1612 and the monument was installed 10 years later.

7 | *(left)* Interior of The Royal Exchange, 1788. This was the second building on the site.

'diversity advantage'. As the French philosopher Voltaire wrote in 1764, belief was no bar to doing business in London's Royal Exchange:

> There the Jew, the Mahometan, and the Christian bargain with one another as if they were of the same religion, and bestow the name of infidel on bankrupts only. There the Presbyterian gives credit to the Anabaptist, and the votary of the establishment accepts the promise of the Quaker. On the separation of these free and pacific assemblies, some visit the synagogue, others repair to the tavern.

There is no doubt that philanthropy in the City was party driven by the values of its non-Anglican families and firms. The roll-call of City philanthropists includes Quakers, such as Elizabeth Fry (1780–1845) and Peter Bedford (1780–1864), alongside members of the City's Jewish community, among them Lionel Louis Cohen (1832–1888) and Samuel Montagu (1832–1922). Altogether, the strong sense of community obligation within Dissenting and Jewish circles combined with the confidence of the Anglican establishment, and indeed the Protestant work ethic, to embed charity in the City's daily life.

The final thread in the City's philanthropic DNA is the link with the more practical side of business: organisational models and financial methods. Charitable enterprise needs to marshall its resources in a business-like way, and the City has been the place where skills and ideas have naturally travelled from one sphere of activity to the other. It has offered mechanisms for managing charitable bequests in the long term; together with a pool of individuals with an entrepreneurial frame-of-mind and the financial skills required for organisational good governance.

London's citizens thus had the means, motives and methods to do good. But the choice to act was of course a personal one. For the individual citizen, whether Tudor widow or Victorian stockbroker, charity must have made sense. For some it may have been purely a pious duty, for others it represented civic contribution, political advantage or a sense of moral outrage. Whatever the motive, individual actions have added up to a collective story about the City which has delivered long-lasting change to London.

8 | Soup kitchen for the Jewish Poor: new premises opened in Brune Street in 1903, with funding from Lord Rothschild and Sir Samuel Montagu.

LONDON BRIDGE

London Bridge testifies to the role philanthropy has played in the City, and its perhaps unexpected associations with utilities and infrastructure.

A bridge across the River Thames has existed since Roman times. In 1176 work started on a new bridge, this one built of stone. Completed in about 1209, the upkeep of the stone bridge became a charitable cause in its own right. Many citizens left gifts of money or land to the bridge's 'estate', swelling the rent and tolls that made up the sinking fund for repairs.

The sums left to the bridge accumulated over the years to form the Bridge House Estate trust fund, managed by the City Corporation. Maintenance of the City's five bridges remains the fund's main objective, but since 1995, surplus monies have been diverted to charitable causes via the City of London Corporation's charity, the City Bridge Trust. Today, City Bridge Trust provides grants totalling around £16 million per year towards charitable activity in Greater London.

9 | Model of Old London Bridge, made *c.*1910.

THE CITY'S HOSPITALS

The most prominent good causes in the early City were its five hospitals. All five sprang from religious houses but passed into the City's care during the suppression of the monasteries, as gifts from Henry VIII. Four hospitals stood within the city boundaries: St. Bartholomew's, Bethlem, Bridewell and Christ's. The fifth, St. Thomas's, was in Southwark.

St. Bartholomew's and St Thomas's provided for the general sick. Bridewell was the place for the vagabond poor. Bethlem specialised in the care of the mentally ill. Originally the Hospital of St Mary of Bethlehem, it stood near today's Liverpool Street Station. In 1675 the City erected a prestigious new building for the hospital at Moorfields, part of the rebuilding that followed the 1666 Great Fire. The new building was proclaimed to be 'a Prime Ornament of the City... and a noble Monument to Charity'.

Christ's Hospital in Newgate Street was re-founded in 1552 as a school for the orphans of freemen. It was the original blue-coat school and pupils wore a distinctive uniform [fig. 15]. Girls were admitted from the start: in 1563, the register listed 132 girls out of 396 children. Christ's remained at its City site until 1902 when the school moved to its present home in Horsham.

10 | *(left)* Donor acknowledgments in the Great Hall at Bart's Hospital: names from 1788 include William Wilberforce and Henry Hoare.

11 | *(above)* Sir Rowland Hill (1495–1561), surveyor-general of the City's hospitals from 1559. His will gave a dole of 12d to every house in the City.

12 | The Great Hall at Bart's Hospital, 1738, fitted out with boards recording the hospital's donors and officers. The boards continued to be installed until 1905. Through the far door is a glimpse of William Hogarth's large paintings in the staircase hall, created for the hospital in 1735–7 for no fee.

the treble people of Cryste
that shalle se or here tho

Philip Malpas at his decease gave one hundred and twenty pounds to poor prisoners, and every year for five years four hundred and three shirts and smocks, forty pairs of sheets, and one hundred and fifty gowns of frieze to the poor; to poor maids' marriages one hundred marks; to highways one hundred marks; and to five hundred poor people in London every one six shillings and eight pence.

John Stow, 1603, describing a bequest of 1439

The City's charitable development mirrors the growth of the City itself as a self-governing entity. As its civic institutions began to take shape from the twelfth century onwards, citizens were exhorted to contribute to the common good. Many did so by giving charitable alms to the Church or undertaking charitable actions, most commonly through bequeathing land or money from which a future income could be generated. Bequests were usually intended to relieve the suffering of the poor, but some were for more practical purposes such as repairing church or monastic buildings. London had some of the most well-endowed monasteries of its day, and many attracted donations during the lifetime of the donor. At the Charterhouse, the Carthusian monastery on the northern borders of the City, the water system was paid for by a London grocer, William Symes.

As the City developed, so two secular alternatives emerged as ways of managing charitable bequests in perpetuity. On the one hand the mayor and aldermen could hold money in trust. The concept of a 'common good' was understood, along with the concept of 'the Mayor and Commonalty' as a collective entity expected to last. Mayors and aldermen already undertook works of public benefit, including the upkeep of London's single bridge and the maintenance of an adequate water supply through public conduits. Thomas Ilam was one of many civic officers who contributed to the water systems: in 1480 he 'newly built the great conduit in Cheape [Cheapside] of his own charges'.

13 | *(opposite)* Dick Whittington on his death bed, surrounded by his executors and the inmates of his almshouse. The image is from the founding document of the almshouse, 1442.

S.ʳ RICH.ᵈ WITTINGTON, *from an Original Painting at MERCERS HALL.*

CHRIST'S HOSPITAL.

14 | *(far left)* Portrait of Richard Whittington, engraved in 1766, several centuries after his death; his enduring fame rested in part on his public works.

15 | *(left)* Engraving of a Christ's Hospital scholar, 1824.

Care of the City's orphaned children also lay with the collective body. A longstanding 'custom of the city' saw the mayor and alderman taking on responsibility for the orphans of freemen. This took institutional form with the 1552 re-foundation of Christ's Hospital as a foundling school, a place where 'poor fatherless children be there brought up and nourished at the charges of the citizens'. Christ's Hospital became one of the City's top charitable causes, attracting a steady stream of endowments and donations. It should be said that the City's guardianship of its orphans was not wholly disinterested, since any property belonging to the orphans was also entrusted to the city chamberlain for safe-keeping: a useful source of capital for the embryonic corporation.

The other secular route for charitable action was through the livery companies. When the humanist cleric John Colet founded St Paul's School in 1509, he did so through the Mercers' Company, famously entrusting them with his charitable legacy on the grounds that he found 'the least corruption' in such a body of citizens. The attraction of the livery companies was not just to avoid the misappropriation of funds by corrupt clerics. As the historian Ian Archer has described:

> The incorporated status of the companies was attractive to those seeking to establish charities in perpetuity... The enjoyment of a legal personality meant that the companies could sue and be sued in the courts, an important consideration for donors who wanted insurance against fraudulent executors.

Dick Whittington [figs. 13, 14] was one example of a merchant who saw secular institutions as the best long-term bet. The foundation ordinances of his almshouses, drawn up in 1424, specified that the future overseers should be both the City Corporation and the Mercers' Company. The responsibility was to be shared jointly between 'the Mayor of the City of London that now is and all his successor Mayors or keepers of the said City... [and] the keepers of the commonalty of the craft or mercerie of London that now be, and all their successor keepers of the same craft'.

The tumultuous changes brought by the Reformation boosted the livery companies'

16 | Crest of the Grocers' Company, a roof corbel from Crosby Hall in Bishopsgate, built 1466–71.

credentials as safe and impeccably Protestant havens for charitable bequests. Located here, charities could be demonstrated as triumphantly Godly, rational and useful. In the 100 years between the 1530s and the 1630s many London citizens responded to the spirit of the age, endowing an abundance of almshouses, schools, and colleges; and leaving the livery companies with an extensive range of new responsibilities. Ian Archer quotes a 1621 letter from the Ironmongers' Company, slightly complaining that their new obligations 'to discharge our consciences in performing the will of the dead' has left them with some unwelcome 'much trouble and hazard'.

DONORS AND CAUSES

Alice Smith, of London, widow, late wife of Thomas Smith of the same City… bequeathed lands to the value of £15 by the year for ever, to the company of Skinners, for the augmenting of the pensions of certain poor, inhabiting in eight alms houses, erected by Sir Andrew Jud, Knight, her father in the parish of Great St Helen's in Bishopsgate Street in London.
John Stow, 1603

What about the donors? Who were these early City philanthropists? Perhaps inevitably, they were the wealthy citizens – which usually meant merchants. As John Stow remarked, 'the private riches of London resteth chiefly in the hands of the merchants and retailers, for artificers have not much to spare and labourers have need that it were given unto them.' The description 'merchant' covered several levels of status. At one end of the scale was the modest dealer in cloth; at the other were the City's oligarchs, men of colossal wealth and fortune. With the loosening of strictures on money lending in the 1570s 'merchant' also came to include financiers, men who seized the opportunites for political wheeling and dealing to become the Tudor equivalent of the super-rich.

Two such were Thomas Gresham, the financial agent of the English crown in the Netherlands; and Thomas Sutton, known to his contemporaries as 'Croesus', 'Rich

17 | The 'Common Chest', early 15th century, made to hold the City's valuables and vital documents.

21

THOMAS GRESHAM (c.1519–1579)

Thomas Gresham was a London merchant and financier whose career was spent in the trading networks between London and Europe, particularly the Low Countries.

Gresham was the son of a former mayor, Sir Richard Gresham. He became a member of the Mercers' Company in 1543 but worked primarily from Antwerp, where he acted as a financial agent and quasi-ambassador for the English Crown. His wealth came from negotiating loans and trading money, arms and goods.

In 1565 Gresham offered to build at his own expense a trading space for London's merchants, modeled on the Antwerp *bourse*. This was the Royal Exchange. On his death he entrusted his estate jointly to the Mercers' Company and the Corporation with the aim of founding a college in London. Originally accommodated in his own house in Bishopsgate, Gresham's College provided for seven professors to give public lectures in astronomy, geometry, physic, law, divinity, rhetoric and music. Today, Gresham College continues to deliver its founder's vision through a programme of free public lectures.

18 | *(left)* Thomas Gresham, painted in 1544.

19 | *(above)* Barnard's Inn, Holborn, the current home of Gresham College.

THOMAS SUTTON (1532 – 1611)

The greatest and noblest gift that was ever given for charity, by any one man, public or private, in this nation
Daniel Defoe, 1726

Thomas Sutton, was a Lincolnshire man by origin, who amassed an enormous fortune during the turbulent years of Queen Elizabeth I's reign. He dealt in weapons, owned coal mines in County Durham and lent money to the Crown. In London he had a town house at Broken Wharf and a grander residence at Stoke Newington.

Sutton's will of 1611 created 'King James Hospital in Charterhouse', an almshouse for over 80 elderly men and a school for 40 poor scholars. It opened in 1614 and was by some margin, the wealthiest charity of its day, both admired and criticised for its ambitious scale.

400 years later, Sutton's grand project is still going strong. Charterhouse School moved out of London in 1872. But the original site remains home for over 40 elderly men: 'the Brothers'. At every lunchtime a Grace is recited, giving thanks to God for Thomas Sutton's foresight and generosity.

20 | *(left)* Thomas Sutton, painted in 1657.

21 | *(above)* Wash-house Court in the Charterhouse, 2013.

Sutton' and 'a mighty monied-man'. Sutton's personal fortune began with his involvement in the Northumberland and Durham coal-trade (he is said to have transported cash by the waggon-load back to London). Both Sutton and Gresham ultimately chose to dispose of their colossal personal wealth with public benefit in mind. Gresham's legacy included the foundation of London's first proto-university, Gresham College, which still operates today. Sutton established a hospital and school in the Charterhouse, the former mansion of the 4th Duke of Norfolk and his heirs in Smithfield. The Charterhouse was the most lavishly-endowed charity of its day. Hailed by some as 'a Master-piece of Protestant English Charity', it also attracted criticism as an exercise in vanity and money-laundering – an early example of the controversy that can surround philanthropy.

Interestingly, Sutton did not use the livery companies to manage his legacy. He preferred the mechanism of an independent foundation, which was established by the terms of his will under the patronage of the Crown and the Archbishop of Canterbury. Gresham took a more conventional City route, entrusting the future care of his College jointly to the Corporation and the Mercers' Company.

London's philanthropists of this era were not just men. Diverting wealth into charitable undertakings was often the decision of wives, daughters and widows. In 1530 Joan Bradbury left a large estate in what is now Covent Garden, to the Mercers' Company. The land is still owned by the Mercers, whose charitable activities today are largely financed by the rents received from Joan Bradbury's gift. The Mercers' Company also discharged the charitable wishes of Lady Jane Mico, the wife of Sir Samuel Mico – a merchant trading with the Mediterranean. On her death in 1670 Joan Mico left £1,500 to found an almshouse in Stepney for poor widows over the age of 50. Lady Mico's Almshouse was built in 1691 and continues to operate today as a sheltered housing complex in the London Borough of Tower Hamlets. The Trust is still managed by the Mercers' Company.

Thomas Sutton's Foundation of 1611 set a new standard for charitable ambition. It was

22 | *(far left)* The earliest-known Mercers' Maiden property mark, dated 1669, in Corbet Court off Gracechurch Street.

23 | *(left)* A Mercers' Maiden in Long Acre, Covent Garden, marking the land given to the Mercers by Joan Bradbury in 1530.

said of Sutton in 1737 that his was the largest fortune diverted to charitable ends 'until the Indian wealth dispersed through Europe, the Public Fund, Paper Credit and other modern methods have given some persons opportunities of amassing prodigious riches'. The writer was perhaps thinking of Thomas Guy (1644–1724), often described as a bookseller and printer but also a City oligarch who had amassed his prodigious riches through dealing in South Sea stock. In 1721 Guy bought a plot of land in Southwark on which to build a hospital. The new institution was intended by its founder to compete with the nearby St Thomas's Hospital, to which Guy had also given money but with whom he had fallen out. Guy's Hospital opened in 1726.

The other prodigiously rich City benefactor of the day was Sir John Cass (1661–1718). Cass was a one-time Member of Parliament for the City, he was also a sheriff and alderman for Portsoken Ward, the place of his birth. He was a High Church Tory-Anglican, sometime Master of the Carpenters' and Skinners' companies and deeply engaged in the Corporation's factional politics. In 1709 he founded an independent charity school (having already generously supported the parochial school) in Portsoken ward, which was endowed by the terms of his will but unable to benefit from the endowment until legal wranglings had run their course. The Cass Foundation was finally established in 1748 and, today, is the City's most active independent educational charity, supporting not just the original school, but also several university departments, a halls of residence and an outdoor centre. Altogether, eight institutions bear the name of Cass, which is also attached to a great range of educational activities throughout London.

24 | *(above)* Bust of Sir John Cass in St Botolph Bishopsgate by Eric Winter, 1966, but after a 1751 statue by Roubiliac.

25 | *(left)* Charity children statues at the Sir John Cass Foundation Primary School, Duke's Place.

26 | Charity children statues at *(below)* St. Andrew Holborn, Holborn Viaduct; and *(right)* St Bride's, Fleet Street.

CHARITY SCHOOLS

Charity schools, as they developed in the late seventeenth century, were small local institutions, run by the parish or ward 'for teaching poor children to read, write and other necessary parts of education'. They began as a London phenomenon, partly modelled on Christ's Hospital School, and spread rapidly. By the 1720s there were over 130 charity schools in the London region.

London's charity schools tended to be fervently Anglican, and the highspot of the year was the annual anniversary meeting of the charity schools of London, Westminster and Southwark at St Paul's Cathedral. The tradition began around 1710 and by the early nineteenth century 8,000 children were being accommodated on scaffolding stands within the Cathedral. The service was preceded by a procession through the streets, a collection was taken after the service, and constables were employed to manage the watching crowds.

'A more glorious sight, or one that a nation can be prouder of, is not to be seen in the whole world', said a correspondent to *The Times* in 1825, who went on to criticize the expense.

27 | The anniversary meeting of charity school children at St Paul's Cathedral, by Robert Havell Junior, 1826.

THE LONDON HOSPITAL, E.1.

THE LONDON HOSPITAL
FOUNDED 1740.

GUY'S HOSPITAL, S.E.1.

AMBULANCE

Save your Hospitals

SOCIETIES AND SUBSCRIPTIONS

Thus might Charity, Humanity, Patriotism and Economy be made to go hand in hand.

John Massie, 1758

Methods of funding charitable enterprise began to change in the eighteenth century, reflecting changes in business practice. Endowments of landed wealth or cash gave way to 'associated philanthropy' – raising money through joint subscriptions or incorporated companies. These changes coincided with a new mood of 'Enlightenment' values, a frame of mind that strove for modernisation and improvement in all aspects of social and economic life. The aims of charity moved closer to the aims of commerce: both sought to advance Britain's national interest through creating a healthy and prosperous population.

This is the period when the word 'philanthropy' starts to emerge alongside 'charity' as a way of describing benevolent action. Chambers' *Cyclopaedia* of 1728 defined philanthropy as 'a love of mankind; a general benevolence towards the species', and the word came to be applied to people engaged in campaigning for humanitarian causes, as well as people leaving bequests of money or subscribing to institutions. Among the new type of social-justice philanthropists were many men and women from commercial or dissenting backgrounds. Prominent Quaker philanthropists of the day included Elizabeth Fry (1780–1845), who campaigned for prison reform from her home in Mildred Court, and William Allen (1770 – 1843) whose pharmacy in Plough Court became meeting places for many humanitarian campaigns, including those concerned with the abolition of slavery and the slave trade.

The climate of improvement and enlightenment created a new generation of London hospitals and orphanages with governance arrangements that reflected new business practices. The banker Henry Hoare (1677 – 1725) was one of the 'well-disposed gentlemen' behind the foundation of the Westminster Infirmary in 1720, the first

28 | *(opposite)* Two posters produced by the King's Fund, 1923, as part of a fund-raising campaign.

ELIZABETH FRY.

29 | *(far left)* Elizabeth Fry (1780 – 1845).

30 | *(left)* William Allen (1770 – 1843).

hospital in England to be maintained entirely by annual subscriptions. Associated philanthropy suited the City's way of doing business well. Subscribers met face-to-face at coffee houses, churches and meeting houses. Fund-raising was easily combined with public sociability in the form of concerts, assemblies and dinners. The London Hospital, which followed the Westminster Infirmary's model of subscription funding, began with a meeting of interested parties at the Feathers Tavern in Cheapside in 1740. The City of London Lying-in Hospital was founded at a meeting in the Black Swan Tavern in Bartholomew Lane.

One of the most prominent of the new institutions was Thomas Coram's Foundling Hospital, which opened on a green-field site above Holborn in 1741. The hospital was initially financed by subscriptions, and the historian Donna Andrew has pointed out that City merchants and financiers were prominent among its subscribers and governors:

> not only were such men able and willing to contribute money and financial
> expertise to the operation of the charity, but their large circle of business
> acquaintances included many potential subscribers, who could be persuaded to
> contribute and serve the charity in times of need.

The City factor did not, unfortunately, bring stability to the Foundling Hospital's financial arrangements. In 1756 an appeal to Parliament generated a £10,000 annual grant from national government for the institution, but with strings attached. The grant was discontinued four years later, but in the meantime the Hospital had discovered an alternative method of raising funds. Concerts conducted by the composer George Frideric Handel produced a regular source of income until Handel's death in 1759.

Philanthropic efforts were not necessarily focussed on institutions. An outburst of new societies occurred around 1800, promoting campaigns or causes. The Society for the Suppressing of Vice campaigned against ungodly behaviour. The Society for the Discharge and Relief of Persons Imprisoned for Small Debts was founded in 1808 to

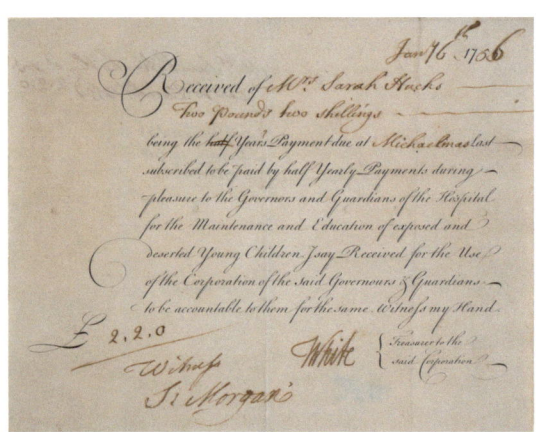

31 | Receipt for a year's subscription to the Hospital for Exposed and Deserted Children (Thomas Coram's Foundling Hospital), 1756.

32 | (opposite) A City Chop-House by Thomas Rowlandson, c.1810–15.

campaign for legal and penal reform; the promoters acting 'not merely from the avowed humanity of its purpose, but also... from the advancement which it afforded to society at large'. In a published account of their work, the Committee recorded their animation at their initial success: 'expectations were more highly received when they perceived what GREAT EVENTS from LITTLE CAUSES might succeed'.

One of the City's most interesting philanthropic experiments of the era was the Meat and Soup Charity, established to 'better the condition of the labouring people... particularly in the City of London and its environs'. The charity was established by a Committee at Lloyds Coffee House, a group which had set up as something of a think-tank about poverty as well as a vehicle for raising funds 'for the relief of the out-parishes'. Members included the merchant and underwriter John Julius Angerstein, whose art collection later formed the nucleus of the National Gallery. The scheme was entrusted to the magistrate Patrick Colquhoun, a zealous deviser of social improvement schemes – most famously his invention of the Thames River Police.

The aim of the Soup Charity was not just to provide temporary relief, but also 'to allure the labouring population into a better, cheaper and more wholesome mode of preparing their food'. It aimed to do this through a dauntingly complex system, requiring tickets, vouchers, chits and countersigned certificates of recommendation, to be passed from superintendents to parish beadles to the cooks in the Eating Houses enrolled in the scheme. The quantity of paper transactions perhaps could be seen as reflecting the methods of doing financial business that the scheme's promoters knew so well. The scheme was described as an 'experiment', but despite procuring a large store of potatoes, training cooks, appointing superintendents and issuing 181,276 tickets for Leg of Beef soup (and 24,889 tickets for potatoes) between February and July 1797, the experiment was not repeated.

The institutions that emerged from the spirit of metropolitan improvement reflected the optimism of the age. London was now an astonishing metropolis, a new Rome, the envy of the world. Orphanages and hospitals expressed national and civic pride

LONDON ORPHAN ASYLUM, CLAPTON.

33 | The London Orphan Asylum, a print from *Metropolitan Improvements* by T. H. Shepherd, 1828.

through their classical architecture and lavish scale. A Polish writer, Krystyn Lach-Szyrma, visiting in the mid-1820s, noted that:

> England is famous among all nations for its charity institutions. There is no distress, trouble or disability which is not the concern of some charity... The few institutions founded by government are antiquated; the private foundations are far more numerous.

Around the City, the new buildings included the London Orphan Asylum in Clapton, constructed between 1820 and 1825, and the Royal Caledonian Institution in Islington built to house orphans of Scottish soldiers. In both cases, grand, classical porticos proclaimed the institutions to be vehicles for the enlightened values of modern civilisation. Even the older institutions caught the spirit of the age. Bethlem Hospital was transformed into a neo-classical palace when it moved from Bishopsgate to Lambeth in 1815.

Although the new hospitals and asylums presented themselves as splendid public institutions, they were never designed for mass use. Demand far outstripped supply, particularly for institutions caring for children. A selection process decided who would be admitted to their care. Thomas Coram's Foundling Hospital famously held a ballot as a way of allocating places. The London Orphan Asylum held an annual election, with an institution's subscribers and governors entitled to vote on which child should be admitted. G E Hicks' picture of 1865 captures the event, held at the London Tavern in Bishopsgate. The Museum of London's collections also contains a tiny 'election flyer' which urges governors to vote for Elizabeth Rose Shepherd, the 7-year-old orphan-daughter of a Kent solicitor.

Besides supporting new institutions and societies, City residents continued to respond to appeals for funds to help relieve the suffering of the poor. Most winters saw an appeal, or 'subscription', on behalf of the distressed Spitalfields weavers. The names of those who responded were published in *The Times*, where the lists of subscribers were set out under the names of the City's banks which acted as collecting

34 | *An Infant Orphan Election at the London Tavern: Polling,* by G. E. Hicks, 1865.

35 | (top) '£.s.d. The Accepted
Religion of England', cartoon from
*The Tomahawk: A Saturday
Journal of Satire*, February 1870.

36 | (above) 'Our London Poor: a
tea for 700 tramps and beggars in
Moorgate Street Hall', *The Graphic*,
15 Jan 1876.

points. The 1816 appeal solicited 11 donations *via* Messrs Hoare of Fleet Street, including the partners themselves who gave £100 – the largest single sum. Other donors included Sir George Osborn, who gave £50; and two anonymous children, who gave 5 shillings 'from their reward money'. The patronage of the Lord Mayor added weight to the Spitalfields' appeals. By the mid- nineteenth century the 'Mansion House Fund' was raising money for disasters further afield: the West Indies hurricane in 1867, the Bengal famine in 1874 and the Hungarian floods in 1879.

CONTROVERSY AND REFORM

Indiscriminate charity is among the curses of London… I would say that the poor starve because of the alms they receive.
Samuel Barnett, 1874

Philanthropy was never more controversial than in late-Victorian London. As the gap between rich and poor in the nation's capital became wider and more alarming, so efforts to address deteriorating urban conditions became more frantic. It was no longer just Spitalfields that gave cause for concern: the labouring population across the whole East End appeared to be at risk of falling into the 'abyss'. The rich were exhorted to give more, but also accused of tinkering with poverty's symptoms rather than its causes. Philanthropy was caught up in the bitter debate about whether the State should assume responsibilities for poor relief. Was a reinvigorated Church the answer? Did gifts from rich to poor make matters worse by turning workers into paupers? Were philanthropists standing in the way of solutions? Meanwhile conditions in London's poorer districts continued to deteriorate.

The City was at the heart of the controversy. The 1886 Mansion House appeal to relieve distress in the metropolis became notorious. Despite raising a colossal £78,000, it was bitterly criticised for the indiscriminate distribution of 'doles'. The professional charity organiser Octavia Hill spoke of the 'terrible mistakes and failures' of the Mansion House Fund: 'if the money had been thrown into the sea, it would have been better'.

37 | Hoare's Bank in Fleet Street, 2013. The bank occupies its original site, and has developed a strong tradition of philanthropy over the centuries.

But yet the nineteenth century also saw what was arguably one of the City's most far-reaching, philanthropic success stories: housing. Then, as now, housing for London's working population was an intractable problem, and it was the City where the challenge was taken up most vigorously. The vehicle favoured by housing-philanthropists was the '5% philanthropy' company, where good causes went hand-in-hand with a return on investment. Sidney Waterlow's Improved Industrial Dwellings Company began building blocks of flats in 1865. Waterlow (1822–1906) was a City figure, a Liberal politician and one-time Lord Mayor whose printing firm supplied the Square Mile's financial industry with its specialist stationery. A similar initiative was the 4% Industrial Dwellings Society, formed in 1885 by a group of Jewish philanthropist-bankers and investors, led by the first Lord Rothschild (1840–1915).

The City's most famous housing-philanthropist was the American banker, George Peabody (1795–1869). In 1862 Peabody set up a Trust to 'ameliorate the condition of the poor and needy' of the 'great metropolis of London', which it decided to achieve through building tenement flats on a very large scale. The Trust soon became the most important provider of mass-housing in the capital, often building on cleared land bought from the Metropolitan Board of Works at a knock-down price. Peabody estates provided sanitary but spartan accommodation in areas such as Spitalfields and Clerkenwell where overcrowding was becoming notorious.

Housing schemes of this sort did not escape the criticism that increasingly attached to philanthropy. The estates erected by the new housing companies were for the sort of workers that made up the City's own workforce, rather than the very poor whose situation was so distressing. Peabody's work was criticized for this, but whatever the approach, the achievement was undeniable. Peabody was honoured by the City during his life time with a statue erected outside the Royal Exchange [fig. 8].

A second philanthropist who was celebrated in her life time, but who also attracted controversy, was Angela Burdett-Coutts – the richest woman in England. Burdett-Coutts' charitable interests were famously idiosyncratic yet by no means out-of-touch

38 | (*far left*) Navarino Mansions, Hackney, built by the 4% Industrial Dwellings Company, 1903–5.

39 | (*left*) Waterlow Buildings, Bethnal Green, built 1869–90.

GEORGE PEABODY (1795 – 1869)

He was a philanthropist who was liked as well as honoured. There was nothing hard or narrow about his philosophy. He simply did whatever good came his way.
    Anonymous writer on George Peabody, 1896

George Peabody was born in America and began his business career in Baltimore as an importer of British goods. Frequent trips to London persuaded him to move his operations to the British capital and by 1838 he was living and working in the City with offices at 31 Moorgate Street. During the 1840s George Peabody & Co., moved into finance, dealing in American railroad stock.

Despite a crisis in 1857, the firm prospered and by the 1860s George was devoting his time and wealth to charitable enterprises. His 'Peabody Donation Fund', later the Peabody Trust, began building tenement blocks for London's workers in 1862 and within a few years the distinctive Peabody estates had become familiar sights in inner-city London.

Peabody is said to have refused the offer of a Baronetcy. He was a modest man, with an unassuming lifestyle, according to the anonymous author of *Four Great Philanthropists* (1896): 'pastry or cake he seldom indulged in, but he was very fond of fruit.'

ANGELA BURDETT-COUTTS (1814–1906)

The Lady Bountiful of our time ...
Blanchard Jerrold, 1872

Baroness Burdett-Coutts was famous during her life time as the richest woman in England. She inherited her great wealth from her grandfather, a partner in Coutts' Bank. Motivated in part by her faith, she devoted her life to charitable activity – which by the time of her death amounted to £3 million-worth of donations and projects. She had an entrepreneurial approach to philanthropy, financing schemes of her own devising, as well as financing those drawn up by others. Her good causes included model dwellings, soup kitchens, drinking fountains, shoe-black brigades, ragged schools, the RSPCA, bee-keeping and church building.

Burdett-Coutts worked closely with the City Corporation, particularly over the Columbia Road housing and market complex she built in Bethnal Green. Here, the tenement flats were specifically intended to provide housing for City workers. She was the first woman freeman of the City of London and the first woman to be raised to the peerage in her own right.

Today, her work in the East End of London is commemorated in several street names: Baroness Road and Georgina Gardens on the Columbia Market site (Georgina was her middle name), and Burdett Road, in Bow.

41 | Angela Burdett-Coutts,
a print published in *Vanity Fair*, 1883.

with the main issues of the day. The blocks of flats she erected at Columbia Road, Bethnal Green, responded to the flurry of activity and debate around urban housing. The tenements fulfilled their purpose but the accompanying Columbia Market was an ill-conceived scheme. Opened to great fanfare in 1869, the great Gothic pile was intended to transform the lives of street-trading costermongers by providing respectable, indoor facilities. But high rents and impractical trading arrangements meant that the costermongers remained on the streets. When the building failed to function as planned, the City Corporation stepped-in with the aim of running it as a fish-market, supplying the people of the East End with nutritious food. However, planned railway- lines were not built and four years later the Corporation handed the building back to its creator.

The debate surrounding charity in late Victorian London did not inhibit the time-old practice of leaving a bequest in a will. In 1881, the will of William Ward, a City merchant who lived at Brixton Hill, left £20,000 'to the Mayor and Commonalty of the City of London for the purposes of founding a high school for girls to be known as "The City of London School for Girls, founded by William Ward" and to correspond as near as may be with the City of London School for Boys'. Ward also left the residue of his estate to the City Corporation 'for the purposes of erecting and maintaining some institution or creating a fund for the benefit of the poorer classes'. Ward's reference point, the City of London School for Boys, had opened some decades earlier in 1837 using funds accumulated from the bequest of John Carpenter in 1442. Both schools, for girls and boys, remain in the City today.

At the time of Ward's bequest, the intense debates around poverty and social reform were becoming entangled with equally bitter debates about London's government, and the role of the City Corporation in the light of the expected creation of a new London County Council. All this threw a spotlight on the City churches and their ancient charitable endowments. There had been long been calls to modernise arrangements for City parishes but by the mid-nineteenth century, change was unavoidable. Population change had left many City parishes without any poor residents to be the

42 | (far left) Angela Burdett-Coutts presenting Columbia Market to the Lord Mayor, 1871.

43 | (left) Angela Burdett-Coutts painted by an unknown artist in 1844.

beneficiaries of charities established centuries earlier. But rising land values meant that the charities were richer than ever. In 1865 the City's parochial charities were generating an annual income of £65,000. Where, people asked, was the money going?

Modernisation came with The City of London Parochial Charities Act of 1883, a landmark in the City's philanthropy story. The Act merged 1,400 moribund charities into a new 'City Parochial Foundation' which began work in 1891 with the purpose of benefitting the 'poorer classes of the Metropolis', i.e. the poor beyond the boundaries of the originating parish. The trustees of the new fund (now 'Trust for London') turned their attention to technical education, a subject close to the hearts of both the City Corporation and the newly-formed London County Council. The City remained London's largest industrial centre, housing a large day-time population of workers in both manufacturing and commerce. Concern about Britain 'falling behind' economically, due to poor levels of skills and unmodernised working practices, were particularly intense in the Square Mile. In response, the City Parochial Foundation began its work by building three new institutes to serve the workforce in the City and surrounding areas. Bishopsgate Institute [fig. 45], Cripplegate Institute and St Bride's Institute were all opened in the 1890s, the latter providing specialist classes and resources for the print trade, then ensconced in Fleet Street.

Technical education was deeply embedded in the City's philanthropic activity throughout the last quarter of the nineteenth century. Another landmark was the creation of the City and Guilds scheme in 1878, a joint endeavour between 16 of the larger livery companies together with the City Corporation. The new scheme was designed to improve workforce skills through examinations, grants and the establishment of new teaching institutions. A central City and Guilds Institute was opened in 1880 at Finsbury, later moving to South Kensington to become the nucleus of Imperial College. Several livery companies founded specialist trade schools: Cordwainers' College (now part of the University of the Arts) began life in 1878 as the Leather Trades School, serving the boot and shoe trade; Goldsmiths College [fig. 45] was opened at New Cross by the Goldsmiths' Company in 1904 as a school of technical

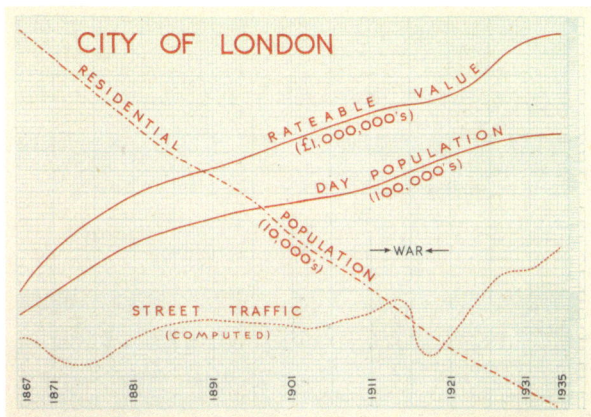

44 | Graph contrasting the City's population fall with its rising land values, published in 1944 as part of the City Corporation's Report on post-war reconstruction.

education and teacher training; the Carpenters' Company established a school in Great Titchfield Street for apprentices in the building trades. Altogether, the livery companies found a re-invigorated sense of purpose in technical education; and their activity in the field helped deflect calls for their disestablishment. They too, like the parish charities, had come under hostile scrutiny as part of the debate about the reform of London government.

The arrival of the new generation of technical schools created many new good causes for would-be philanthropists. It was said in 1890, at a meeting proposing a new Polytechnic Institute in South West London that 'by far the most generous contributors [to similar institutions] had been the wealthy merchants and companies in the City of London'. Indeed, the Polytechnic movement itself had a particularly strong City connection in the person of Quintin Hogg (1845–1903). Hogg was the youngest son of a one-time Director of the East India Company; the family firm was based in Rood Lane. Hogg's tireless educational work included the foundation of the Regent Street Polytechnic, a pioneering institution that became the model for a network of other Polytechnics across London. Hogg's work also helped to build bridges between the City, the livery companies and the newly formed London County Council – which also embarked on a vigorous programme of technical-education institution-building in the 1890s.

By the turn of the century, new areas of philanthropic activity were opening up, alongside technical education. The arts, libraries, museums and green spaces all emerged as progressive causes of the day. Sir Henry Peek (1825–1898), a tea-broker with large warehouses around Eastcheap was instrumental in 'saving' Wimbledon Common as a public space. In 1889 the City Parochial Foundation took over the running of Chelsea Physic Garden from the Society of Apothecaries, averting the closure of Britain's second oldest botanical garden. The Whitechapel Art Gallery opened in 1901 thanks to the support of philanthropists such as John Passmore Edwards (1823–1911), although he withheld his last donation when the gallery refused to name the building after him. Thankfully the missing sum was provided by one of the

45 | *(far left)* Bishopsgate Institute.

(left) Goldsmiths College.

46 | *(top left)* Sculpted frieze of camels on Peek House, Eastcheap, the headquarters of Henry Peek, saviour of Wimbledon Common and Putney Heath.

47 | *(top)* Putney Heath.

48 | *(left)* Whitechapel Art Gallery.

49 | *(above)* Chelsea Physic Garden.

SAVE YOUR HOSPITALS

DEVONSHIRE HOUSE PICCADILLY,
A SALE OF CHRISTMAS DAINTIES
FRI. & SAT. DECEMBER 8th. & 9th.
ALL PROCEEDS GO TO THE HOSPITALS

City's most high-profile, yet subsequently controversial philanthropists, Edgar Speyer (1862–1932), a figure whose reputation was unjustly and maliciously ruined in his life time and which is only just being rehabilitated. Speyer's philanthropy had a lasting impact on the musical life of the capital, not least through saving the Queen's Hall Promenade Concerts. Speyer was one of a group of German financiers, Alfred Beit and Ernest Cassel among them, whose philanthropic contributions to London were immense.

As the twentieth century proceeded, the landscape of philanthropy shifted. New charity laws and the reshaping of the State to take on responsibility for social welfare meant continuous change. New charitable trusts and foundations were formed, many in the wake of Andrew Carnegie (1835 – 1919), whose trust embarked in 1913 on a vigorous programme of improvements to Britain's libraries and universities. Existing voluntary-funded institutions adapted to meet the new opportunities for raising money from an increasingly literate mass public. The City's hospitals embraced modern methods of fundraising, realising that income from their landed endowments was no longer sufficient to meet their needs. In 1897 a new fund, associated with the Prince of Wales but later known as 'The King's Fund', came into being. The Fund provided a central strategic body for London's 127 voluntary hospitals and its initial objective was to enable them to stand on their own two feet: 'if these institutions are to be saved from the State or parochial aid, their financial condition must be secured'.

The King's Fund directed its appeal across the whole spectrum of Londoners: from bankers, who were well represented on the Fund's finance and governing committees; to members of the 'League of Mercy', which focussed on working-class support. In 1922 the Fund embarked on a public appeal, conceived as 'the greatest mass campaign on behalf of hospitals in London's history' and designed in part to restore funds exhausted after the First World War. Fundraising events included flag-days, charity balls, fairs, bazaars, carnivals, ballroom-dancing competitions, concerts, exhibitions and sporting events, plus London's first aerial 'skywriting' advertisements. When completed, the appeal had raised £480,000, slightly less than the target of £500,000.

50 | *(opposite and left)* Posters from the King's Fund's 1922 'Save Your Hospitals' appeal.

Despite these efforts, the move towards the State was inevitable and in 1948 Bart's, along with the City's other hospitals, passed into the National Health Service after 800 years of being 'endowed by the benevolence and charity of the citizens of London'.

The success story of the City's twentieth-century philanthropy was in many ways the livery companies, who adapted to the new climate through a slow but steady process of modernisation, only interrupted by the need to rebuild premises destroyed in the Blitz. By the end of the twentieth century the charitable activities of the livery companies had become thoroughly professionalised, dispensing around £40 million in grants every year. Education continued to be the cause of choice, accounting for 51% of the charitable spend, followed by welfare with 31%. Today London's livery companies have affiliations with 153 schools and academies across Britain, and provide 855 dwellings for the elderly, many managed directly by the companies.

By the end of the twentieth century the focus had once more turned to individuals in the City's workforce. 'Big Bang' of 1986 revolutionised the financial sector's way of doing business, and the expansion of the financial markets that followed generated flows of wealth through the City on a scale unimaginable to Thomas Sutton or George Peabody. But should this wealth be channelled into 'giving something back'? Today, new questions are being asked about philanthropy and the role the rich play in society. Nowhere is this debate more intense that in the City.

As the next chapter outlines, many City firms and individuals have responded imaginatively to the new climate. The aspiration for the City to become 'a global centre for philanthropy' is being realised. Today's buzz around philanthropy rightly looks to the future. But the City's past is a powerful reminder that philanthropy in the City has always been about experiment, excitement and the bounce of creative ideas between business and the voluntary sector. Above all it is a reminder that when the experiments succeed, philanthropy can create long-term gains for the whole of society; and that its effects, both predicted and unpredicted, can last for centuries.

51 | Students on a book-binding course at the London College of Printing, 1965; and Shoreditch College, 1958. Both institutions were supported by the City's livery companies during the 20th century.

52 | Guests, including arts-funders and
philanthropists, at the opening of the Galleries of
Modern London in the Museum of London, 2010.

NOTES AND ACKNOWLEDGMENTS

This essay owes a great deal to the historians whose works are listed below under 'Further Reading'. All quotes from John Stow are taken from the 1603 text of *A Survey of London*, as modernised in the Everyman edition of 1910. The quote from Frederick von Raumer is taken from: Celina Fox, *London – World City, 1800 – 1840* (1992); the quote from Krystyn Lach-Szyrma is taken from *London Observed: A Polish Philosopher at Large, 1822-24* by Krystin Lach-Szyrma and Mona Kedslie McLeod (2009). The author would like to thank: Dominic Tickell of the Charterhouse; Richard Foley of the Sir John Cass Foundation; Jane Ruddell and Donna Marshall of the Mercers' Company; Katie Ormerod of Bart's Hospital; Natasha Ferguson and Sean Waterman of the Museum of London for help with picture research and sourcing images; Lawrence Watson for the photographs and Joe Ewart for the book design.

FURTHER READING

Donna T. Andrew, *Philanthropy and Police: London Charity in the 18th Century*, (Princeton, 1992).

Ian W Archer, 'The Livery Companies and Charity in the Sixteenth and Seventeenth Centuries' in *Society, and Economy in London, 1450 – 1800*, ed. I.A. Gadd and P. Wallis (London: Centre for Metropolitan History, 2002).

Ian W Archer, 'The Charity of Early Modern Londoners' in *Transactions of the Royal Historical Society, sixth series*, 12 (2002), 223-244.

Caroline Barron, *London in the Later Middle Ages*, (Oxford, 2004).

Jean Imray, T*he Charity of Richard Whittington: a History of the Trust administered by the Mercers' Company, 1424–1966* (London, 1968).

W.K. Jordan, *The Charities of London, 1480–1660* (London, 1960).

Stephen Porter, *The London Charterhouse* (Stroud, 2009).

Frank Prochaska, *Philanthropy and the Hospitals of London: The King's Fund, 1897–1990* (Oxford, 1992).

Betsy Rogers, *Cloak of Charity: Studies in Eighteenth-Century Philanthropy* (London, 1949).

GRESHAM
COLLEGE

Founded in 1597

Gresham
College

Free
Public Lectures

Gresham
College

PHILANTHROPY: CITY SITES

The map overleaf shows a small selection of the many hundreds of sites in the City of London with historic associations to philanthropy. The selection includes sites associated with giving and receiving; key institutions and sites linked to significant individuals. Today, some of these sites are marked by commemorative statues or plaques, but many are not.

53 | Pavement plaque in Cheapside, marking the site of the Great Conduit, a public water supply which regularly attracted private funds for its repair over the centuries.

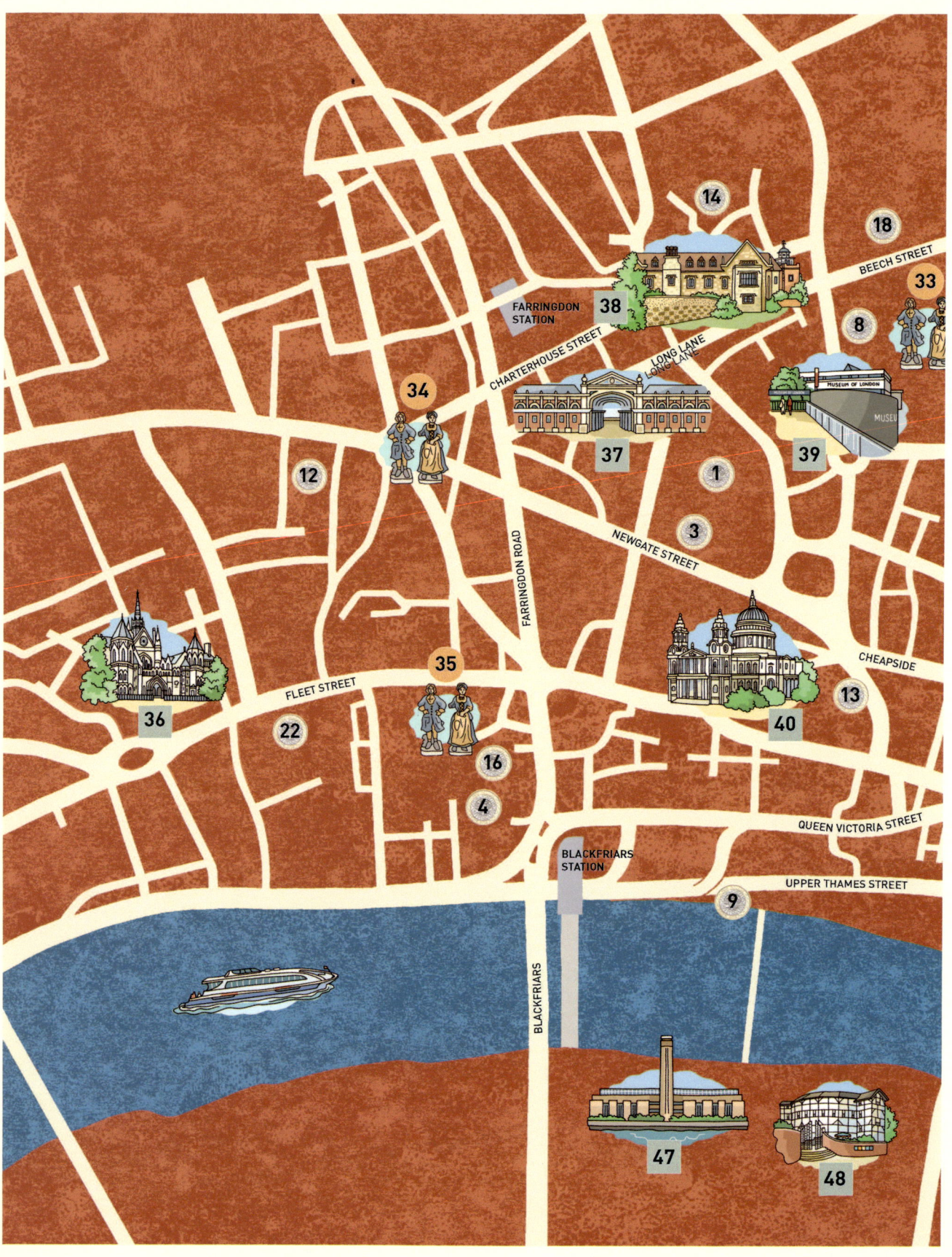

14

18

BEECH STREET

33

FARRINGDON
STATION

38

CHARTERHOUSE STREET

LONG LANE
LONG LANE

8

Museum of London

39

MUSEU

34

37

12

1

3

NEWGATE STREET

FARRINGDON ROAD

CHEAPSIDE

36

FLEET STREET

35

13

22

40

16

4

QUEEN VICTORIA STREET

BLACKFRIARS
STATION

UPPER THAMES STREET

9

BLACKFRIARS

47

48

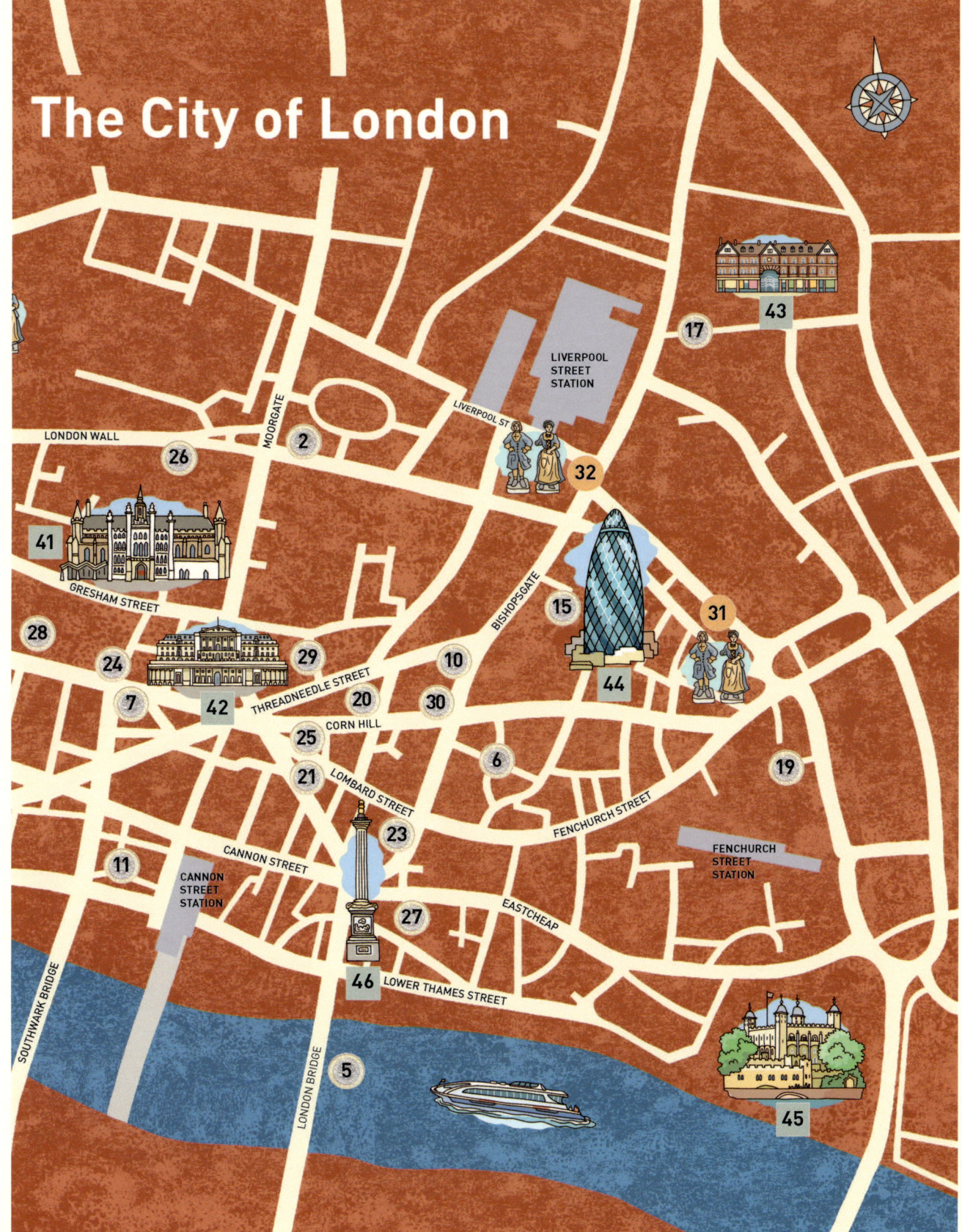

The City of London

LONDON WALL

MOORGATE

GRESHAM STREET

THREADNEEDLE STREET

CORN HILL

LOMBARD STREET

CANNON STREET

BISHOPSGATE

LIVERPOOL ST

LIVERPOOL STREET STATION

FENCHURCH STREET

EASTCHEAP

FENCHURCH STREET STATION

CANNON STREET STATION

SOUTHWARK BRIDGE

LONDON BRIDGE

LOWER THAMES STREET

2
26
41
28
24
7
42
29
25
21
11
23
27
46
5
20
30
10
6
15
44
31
32
17
43
19
45

1 | St Bartholomew's Hospital
Given to London's citizens to maintain in 1546

2 | Bethlem Hospital (site of)
Site of the hospital's magnificent second building, erected 1675-6

3 | Christ's Hospital School (site of)
The City's school for orphans, sited here from 1552 to 1902

4 | Bridewell Hospital (site of)
Given to London's citizens to maintain in 1553. Demolished 1860s

5 | London Bridge
Maintained through tolls and bequests from 1209: the source of funds for the City of London Corporation's charity, City Bridge Trust

6 | Leadenhall Market
Originally built as a public granary and college by Alderman Simon Eyre in 1346

7 | The Great Conduit, Cheapside (site of)
A water source for public use, renewed by Thomas Ilam, 1480

8 | City of London School for Girls
Founded with funds bequeathed for this purpose by William Ward in 1881

9 | City of London School
Founded 1837 using funds originally bequeathed by John Carpenter in 1442

10 | The Merchant Taylor's Almshouse (site of)
The City's first almshouse, founded 1413 through the will of John Chircheman

11 | Whittington's College and Almshouse (site of)
Founded by the Mercers' Company through the will of Richard Whittington, 1424

12 | Gresham's College
Founded 1579 through the will of Thomas Gresham

13 | St Paul's School (site of)
Founded 1512 by John Colet as a free school for 350 poor boys

14 | The Charterhouse
A school and almshouse, founded 1611 through the will of Thomas Sutton

15 | St Helen's Church, Bishopsgate
A cluster of early philanthropists' monuments, including Thomas Gresham's

16 | St Bride's Institute
17 | Bishopsgate Institute
18 | Cripplegate Institute
All 3 institutes built in the 1890s by the City Parochial Foundation (now Trust for London)

19 | The Sir John Cass Foundation
Founded 1748 through the will of Sir John Cass, whose statue stands above the door

20 | George Peabody's Statue
Erected by the City in 1869 to honour the banker and housing philanthropist

21 | N.M. Rothschild & Sons, St. Swithin's Lane
Founded 1811: a bank with a long tradition of philanthropy

22 | Hoare's Bank, Fleet Street
Founded 1672: a bank with a long tradition of philanthropy

23 | William Allen's pharmacy, Plough Court (site of)
Where the Quaker philanthropist worked from the 1790s

24 | Elizabeth Fry's home, Mildred Court (site of)
The home of the Quaker philanthropist from 1805

25 | Thomas Guy's book shop, Lombard Street (site of)
The shop run by the founder of Guy's Hospital from 1668

26 | Waterlow Brothers' offices, London Wall (site of)
Head office of philanthropist Sidney Waterlow's printing firm, 1860s

27 | Peek House, Eastcheap
Head office of philanthropist Henry Peek's tea-importing firm, 1880s

28 | Feathers Tavern, Cheapside (site of)
Where the founders of the London Hospital met, 1740

29 | Black Swan Tavern, Bartholomew Lane (site of)
Where the founders of the City of London Lying-In Hospital met, 1750s

30 | The London Tavern, Bishopsgate (site of)
The place for charity dinners in the nineteenth century

Charity school statues still visible in the City today

31 | Sir John Cass's Foundation Primary School, Duke's Place
32 | St Botolph's Church, Bishopsgate (in the church hall)
33 | The Museum of London (in the galleries)
34 | St Andrew's Church, Holborn
35 | St Bride's Church, Fleet Street (in the church)

Landmarks

36 | The Inns of Court
37 | Smithfield Market
38 | The Charterhouse
39 | The Museum of London
40 | St Paul's Cathedral
41 | Guildhall
42 | The Bank of England
43 | Spitalfields Market
44 | 1, St Mary Axe ('the Gherkin')
45 | The Tower of London
46 | The Monument
47 | Tate Modern
48 | The Globe Theatre

PHILANTHROPY: THE CITY'S PRESENT

Philanthropy may not have returned to a Golden Age, but it could be the silver lining in the storm cloud that has hung over the economy, and particularly the City, in recent years. An age of austerity, a retreating state, the conspicuous gulf between the super-wealthy and very poor, the banking crisis, trading and bonus scandals and the occupation of St Paul's in 2011 have set the scene for a new focus on philanthropy in the Square Mile and beyond. This context has ignited new conversations across the City about how society should arrange itself; where the onus for welfare should lie; who pays for artistic excellence and culture, and the responsibilities private individuals and business must embrace in the social contract.

A new impetus for the City 'to be a part of society, not apart from society', as the Rt Hon. the Lord Mayor of London (2012/13) Alderman Roger Gifford has phrased it, coupled with the particular skills and approaches City professionals can deploy, bring a new optimism and vibrancy to philanthropy in the 21st century. The 2007 *Give and Let Give* report, by The Policy Exchange, which explored how a culture of philanthropy could be built within the financial services industry (FSI), emphasised the special contribution the City can make.

> The skills of today's financiers and entrepreneurs are vital to the development of a philanthropic capital market. There are a growing number of ventures in which the wealth and skills that have made London the world's financial centre are being put to use in imaginative ways to create and distribute philanthropic wealth.

> Properly harnessed, the impetus created by this currently disparate group of initiatives could drive the development of a philanthropic

55 | Stephen Dawson, pioneer of Venture Philanthropy (VP) in the UK and founder of Impetus Trust in 2002.

capital market as vibrant and diverse as the financial market they have sprung from. The FSI therefore has a key role to play in signalling to wider society the need for a more generous and creative culture of philanthropy.

This chapter aims to shine a light on just a few of the many individuals, groups, networks, institutions and businesses playing their part. It celebrates a new iteration of the City's tradition of philanthropy as an extension of capitalism that borrows from business models and principles. Of course, this is not completely new. We have seen in the previous chapter how banking families such as the Hoares and Rothschilds helped found hospitals or created companies that offered investors a financial investment through the provision of social housing. Business and philanthropy are two sides of one coin.

And that said, donations and grant-making remain a major component of the mixed funding model that has kept the charity sector alive in an increasingly hostile economic climate. According to a 2007 CAF report, £2.7 billion was granted to charitable causes by the UK's top 500 trusts and grant-making charities, equivalent to approximately 10% of the UK voluntary sector's income. It is broadly comparable with central government spending of £2.5 billion, and individual donations of around £10 billion according to recent UK Giving reports.

But in the last decade we have experienced a paradigm shift around philanthropy as it becomes conflated with business. 'Philanthrocapitalism', a phrase coined by Matthew Bishop, US Business Editor and New York Bureau Chief of *The Economist*, captures this new thinking in his 2008 book *How Giving Can Save The World*, co-authored with Michael Green, who says:

> In a narrow sense, philanthrocapitalism describes the way that a new generation of individuals and organisations are bringing the techniques of business to their giving and social investing. In a broader sense, philanthrocapitalism is about the way that the leaders of capitalism are recognising that our economic system is not going to be sustainable if it screws up the planet or causes social unrest by leaving millions of people behind.

'Venture philanthropy', 'social enterprise', 'micro-finance', 'social-investment' and 'impact investing' are expressions of this new approach that sit well with a City audience, driven by measurement, risk and return, impact, leverage, innovation and entrepreneurship.

Perhaps one of the first indicators of this shift towards a more data-based philanthropy was the creation of New Philanthropy Capital (NPC) in 2002.

56 | Student mentoring is one service provided by IntoUniversity, a charity that aids disadvantaged youth and is backed by the venture philanthropy Impetus Trust.

Photo courtesy of IntoUniversity

57 | Young people play football organised by Street League, a charity that helps disadvantaged youth and is supported by venture philanthropy non-profit Impetus Trust.

Photo courtesy of Street League

This not-for-profit consultancy and think tank was the brainchild of two City professionals who saw this approach as the way to increase the 'bang' of the philanthropic 'buck'. Economist and then Goldman Sachs partner Gavyn Davies, and his fellow partner Peter Wheeler, hatched the plan in the cafeteria of the investment bank's London headquarters. Reflecting on their decision to found NPC, Davies says:

> In financial markets in the late 1990s there was an enormous industry dedicated to putting capital to use where it gets the highest returns. So why couldn't the same be true of philanthropy? We found there wasn't enough information produced in a hard-headed, independent, high-quality way.

Davies and Wheeler proceeded to find like-minded donors to join them, including international financier and award-winning philanthropist

Harvey McGrath (ex-Man Group and Prudential) and in 2002 NPC was registered and launched as a charity. Since then it has been part of a broader movement seeking to understand how the best charities get to be that way, and how grant-makers, philanthropists and other donors can most effectively support them. It is working with a consortium of organisations including The Charities Evaluation Services and The Association of Charitable Foundations to 'inspire impact' throughout the sector so that charities can better understand the difference they make and communicate that to funders.

VENTURE PHILANTHROPY

At the same time NPC was being established, Venture Philanthropy (VP), which works to build scale and capacity within the sector, arrived in the UK, the result of the dissatisfaction venture capitalist Stephen Dawson experienced with his own giving.

> I was frustrated that I had no idea how effective or efficient charities were and suspected that my money made no real difference to the charities or their beneficiaries. Feedback was nil in almost every case.

It was on retiring from ECI Partners, one of the UK's founding firms of the modern private equity industry that Dawson returned to a *Harvard Business Review* article *Virtuous Capital: What Foundations Can Learn From Venture Capital* that had set him thinking in 1997.

> I began to think about whether there was a way I could transfer my experience investing in small and medium-sized businesses to helping charities in the same way.

59 | ARK's first school in Uganda opened in 2013: students take part in ARK's phonics-based literacy programme.

After a period of research Dawson launched Impetus Trust in 2002 'to provide strategic core funding and expertise to high potential charities', acting as a 'magnifying glass', focussing resources onto an organisation for a finite period of time. After 10 years focussing on the alleviation of poverty, Impetus Trust's 2011/12 Impact Report reveals its portfolio of 16 charities and social enterprises have:

- shown a 39% increase in the average number of people helped
- helped more than 485,000 economically disadvantaged people to access education, skills and jobs
- increased their average income by 19%
- created more than £5m of value in management support, pro bono expertise and grants from Impetus.

Impetus estimates for every £1 it invests, it is able to leverage nearly £4 more of value for its portfolio organisations through the deployment of high-calibre pro bono expertise, partnership investment and additional funds raised. It illustrates exactly what the *Give and Let Give* report highlighted – the City is well-placed and equipped to deploy its skills for the benefit of society.

The Private Equity Foundation (PEF) was established in 2006, connecting money and pro bono business expertise from the private equity community to what they consider are the very best in youth interventions, to increase their impact focussing on the issue of young people Not in

Education, Employment or Training (NEETs). Its five-year impact report, published in September 2012, shows it is achieving a 5x multiplier on investment of £30 million and 39,000 hours of pro bono business support to help change over 97,000 disadvantaged young lives. Former Morgan Grenfell and Deutsche Bank executive Charlie Green, co founder of PEF, speaking on the inspiration to establish the network, says:

> We all knew from our previous dealings with charities that although many organisations have hugely inspiring leadership and great interventions, they are often small-scale and under-capitalised. The best way for us to contribute would be to use both our money and business skills to enable small to medium-sized charities with best-in-class programmes to scale up and grow their operations on a sustainable basis. There was no value we could add to the charities' work on the ground – their compassion or their understanding of their mission – but we could support them to become bigger and better at what they were already doing and deliver far more impact.

In July 2013 Impetus Trust and PEF scaled their own organisations and strengthened the sector through a merger, unusual in the charitable sector. Impetus-PEF is backed by a three-year commitment by global private equity firm Warburg Pincus to make a significant financial contribution and provide high-value pro bono volunteers to support their portfolio. Warburg Pincus' Head of Europe Joseph Schull said:

> We are backing a model that we believe in, which combines financial resources with engaged strategic and operational advice to produce greater social impact over the long-term.

Dawson's long-term vision was 'to drive change not only within the charity, but to inspire change across an entire sector or system'. Ten years on and the evidence points to Dawson's success; VP is now a recognised term and approach, and the industry is growing-up. The European Venture Philanthropy Association (EVPA), established in 2004 to build and monitor the growth and development of the VP industry in Europe, estimates over €1 billion is invested in social purpose organisations. Factary, a research consultancy specialising in strategic philanthropy and fundraising, published a 2011 report on the UK VP movement , showing it is worth more than £1.5 billion and provides more than £50 million in support for non-profits; not huge in the scheme of things but significant and promising. Factary director Chris Carnie believes City-friendly VP will grow in years to come:

> The 'City' group of donors, such as financiers and bankers, have always been a hard bunch to reach for fund-raisers, but the idea of investing charitable funds instead of giving them away appeals to them, and it's an approach they are ready to listen to.

The contribution the hedge fund community has made in the UK and around the world is brilliantly captured in the 2013 report *Contributing to Communities*, from the Alternative Investment Management Association (AIMA), the global hedge fund industry association. It reveals a Titan force that can work on a transformational scale. The hedge fund industry's reputation for lavish gala dinners and macho fund-raising behaviour – that annually raise tens of millions of pounds – perhaps undermines the sector's phenomenal philanthropic achievements.

Absolute Return for Kids (ARK) is the international children's charity founded in 2002 and overseen by a number of UK-based hedge fund managers including Arpad Busson of EIM, Ian Wace and Paul Marshall of Marshall Wace, one of the City's largest funds, and Aurum Funds' Kevin Gundle. ARK runs high-achieving academy schools in deprived areas of three UK cities, establishing eight since 2004, and runs education, healthcare and child protection programmes in Sub-Saharan Africa, India and Eastern Europe. Over 10 years it has raised £180 million and more than 430,000 children have benefited from its programmes. It has also challenged the state education system. Marshall says one of the reasons for founding ARK was to encourage giving among the super-rich whose giving he describes as 'pitiful'.

> Like it or not, the challenge we face is how to get the very well-off to give more. Bankers are the worst offenders. They live in a bubble and don't engage enough with their social responsibility. The best way to encourage the rich to give is to allow them a strategic involvement for their money, which is why the seven of us founded ARK in the first place.

One of the world's most generous philanthropists, hedge fund tycoon Chris Cooper-Hohn, created his own giving strategy by founding The Children's Investment Fund in 2003. He donates 0.5% of assets and an extra 0.5% for every year the fund achieves returns of more than 11% to The Children's Investment Fund Foundation (CIFF), which until September 2013 was run by his wife Jamie Cooper-Hohn. He has given almost £1 billion in the five years to 2011. In one year alone, the couple donated £466 million to their charity. It makes CIFF one of Britain's top 30 charities by income and the biggest charitable contributor from the local hedge fund industry. Even more valuable is its approach, defined by rigour, performance measurement, research, analysis, impact, and leverage. By working strategically at policy level with governments and other partners it has achieved transformational changes on the issues it concerns itself with.

60 | Pilotlight, launched in 2003 to match business leaders with charities and social enterprises across the UK, supports charities like Fitzrovia Youth Action (right). Pilotlight has recruited more than 800 business leaders and 25 City corporate partners to serve as mentors and coaches for over 300 organisations.

Focussing its work in developing countries on five strategic areas, peri-natal mortality, under-nutrition, de-worming, early learning and prevention of mother to child transmission of HIV/AIDS, CIFF made £27 million of grants in 2011 and plans to up this to more than £65 million by 2013 – a 40% increase over five years. Its impact, like all things hedge fund, is grand scale – literally helping to save countries. Jamie Cooper-Hohn says:

> CIFF spent its initial years highly concentrated in the area of HIV/AIDS. It's hard now to believe, but when CIFF was founded, five countries in Africa faced questions to their very survival. It was predicted that there would be 20 million children in Africa orphaned due to AIDS by 2010. Through strategic partnerships and investments both directly in countries and with key global players driving policy norms and resource flows, CIFF assumed a notable role in making AIDS care and treatment accessible to children and their families. The recent data from Zimbabwe for instance, where providing the more effective course of therapy for HIV positive pregnant and lactating women increased from 9% to 81% and new annual infections in children reduced by 47% between 2009 and 2012, provides us with additional confidence in the contribution CIFF has made in this area.

The hedge fund community is male-dominated, but women are holding their own in philanthropy. 100 Women in Hedge Funds (100WHF) is an organisation that through education, professional leverage and philanthropy – its three pillars – is helping women to network, improve communication within the alternative investment industry and make a

61 | A Dragon Award, founded in 1987 by the then Lord Mayor Sir David Rowe-Hame, to celebrate sterling examples of community involvement.

difference to their communities. Founded in 2001 with 100 members, today 100WHF boasts more than 12,000 members in 17 locations across three continents, including London. It has raised more than $30 million for its charities.

In the UK 100WHF will partner with Action on Addiction (2013); WellChild (2014); and The Art Room (2015), as part of The Charities Forum of its patrons The Duke and Duchess of Cambridge and Prince Harry. This reflects 100WHF's three philanthropic themes: mentoring, women's and family health, and education. The increase in publicity generated by Prince William's patronage proved beneficial for both the Duke and the organisation – in 2009 when he first became Patron, £500,000 gross was raised for his nominated charity Centrepoint; double the amount of the previous year's fundraising efforts.

Kristen Eshak Weldon, managing director of Blackstone, is Chair of the Board of 100WHF (London) and oversees its activities in London, Geneva, Zurich, Lugano and Paris. She says:

> Philanthropy has been a core focus of 100WHF since our inception in December 2001 and we have raised close to $30 million globally in aid of the organisations we support. 100WHF enables its members and the broader community to make a difference through a series of global philanthropic initiatives. Through the dedication and hard work of our volunteer members and industry supporters, and their generous donations to its fund-raising efforts, we have made a positive impact on the lives of hundreds of thousands of people in the UK and globally.

> Looking forward, as our industry evolves, we continue to reflect the needs of our members in order to make a difference in the alternatives industry and the broader community. We have a number of exciting upcoming initiatives including a Women on Boards project for members who wish to serve on either a Non-Profit Board or Corporate Board, and our 'Give Back' programme, which offers members an automated solution for matching their financial and time resources to specific 100WHF projects.

The *Contributing to Communities* report highlights that skills, contacts, practical help and strategic thinking are particularly valuable contributions the hedge fund sector makes to communities. KPMG's Rob Mirsky, who founded the UK arm of Hedge Funds Care in 2006 that has since distributed over £730,000 in 26 grants says:

> We're great money managers, and what we can do is take that skill set and help charities run better, and understand whether the people they are giving money to are actually capable of using that money efficiently. Given our specialist skills, we are better placed than anybody to do that.

In 2012 Lloyds Banking Group challenged its 200-strong graduate cohort to raise £1 million for its charity of the year, the Alzheimer's Society. The graduates were tasked with fund-raising, awareness-raising and helping Lloyds improve its service to people affected by the condition.

CORPORATE PHILANTHROPY

Big business has been under fire in recent times, charged with an abdication of duty to the wider community, in failing to pay its share of the tax bill and for not giving enough to charity. *The Company Giving Almanac*, published in July 2013 by the Directory of Social Change (DSC), showed companies give a paltry amount compared to what they make. DSC chief executive Debra Allcock Tyler said at the House of Lord's launch that she was 'truly horrified' by the paucity of giving by business. The Almanac found that the total value of corporate philanthropy to charities was worth between £700 million and £800 million and that the average contribution was worth 0.4% of pre-tax profits overall, with cash donations equal to 0.3 % of pre-tax profits.

Surprisingly perhaps, the report highlighted the generosity of the financial sector. The DSC estimates it accounts for a total of £319 million (cash and in-kind) giving, the largest proportion of any one sector. Author Dr Catherine Walker says of the findings:

> Clearly bankers and financiers need not just to re-establish moral values within their business culture but need to shout about it too. They could give more to social causes, but other businesses sectors should look at the example set by the banks and financial institutions in terms of charitable giving and take note.

The Lord Mayor's Dragon Awards founded in 1987 by the then Lord Mayor Sir David Rowe-Hame, were launched to 'shout about' sterling examples of community involvement each year and to lead by example. In 2012 the Awards received 67 applications across 22 boroughs. The 130 winners

63 | Sadler's Wells Company of Elders, a beneficiary of funding from the City of London Corporation's charity, City Bridge Trust. Members of the dance group, have an average age of 75, are drawn from the community, and have had no formal dance training.

awarded over the years run community schemes that have had major impacts on local employment, environmental and social issues. They show the best corporate philanthropy is no longer the chairman's wife's choice and a handshake across an oversized charity cheque; it is hands-on, long-term and strategically-aligned with business objectives. It's part of a business's DNA, not its PR.

The best examples are authentic, colourful, lively and visionary. They are financially creative, socially innovative, high-leverage and high-impact as these two examples show:

▌ The Andaz Liverpool Street Hotel's Catering Trainee Programme, has supported the work of the Providence Row homeless charity by leading workshops with homeless trainees that lead to accredited Food and Hygiene and safety qualifications. Participants also receive support for social issues that might trigger homelessness such as drug dependency. Since April 2011, 32 trainees have benefited from the programme; eight have progressed into paid employment and six are now in further training.

▌ Body & Soul supports young people and families affected by HIV. They partnered with Red Door Communications (RDC) in 2008 to lead the charity's communications strategy. It trained volunteers to speak to media about the charity's work. Since the pairing began, three young people have spoken publicly at City Hall, four are starring in films, four have been interviewed for press articles and one is taking part in a Channel 4 documentary. The scheme has helped grow participants' confidence as well as educate the public about living with HIV.

There are many hundreds more such schemes run by companies of all sizes

64 | Islington Giving is a collaboration between local funders, authorities and businesses that aims to raise the profile of the borough's poorest citizens living in one of the most affluent neighbourhoods. The City of London Corporation's charity, City Bridge Trust, made a £119,500 grant to the campaign that has so far raised £3 million and is hailed as a blueprint for local giving in London.

and sectors in the City that address issues across the gamut. As the *Company Giving Almanac* highlights, the City is leading the way in corporate philanthropy and has much to build on. Indeed, Heart of the City (HOTC), an organisation funded by the City of London Corporation's charity City Bridge Trust, works with London business to develop and share effective and inspiring Corporate Social Responsibility (CSR) programmes. It has more than 600 members who work committedly with thousands of charities.

Business' contribution is crucial in the light of government cuts. At the 2012 Dragon Awards, the then Lord Mayor Alderman David Wootton said:

> In this tough economic climate, corporate-community engagement is more important than ever. Business has the resource, skills and innovation necessary to support the vital work of community organisations, and create jobs and growth. The Lord Mayor's Dragon Awards recognise and reward projects which are making a real difference to our communities, and building a strong, successful and sustainable City.

Corporate philanthropy also makes business sense. CSR organisations report that it is a crucial differentiator for companies wanting to recruit and retain staff. Nick Wright, of UBS, runs the Swiss Bank's Dragon Award-winning community schemes that focus on enterprise and education and have worked to increase employment in the borough of Hackney from 54% to 69% over the past 25 years. The schemes enjoy a 30% take-up by the firm's employees and its pay roll giving scheme introduced in 1995 matches giving up to £1200 per employee a year. He says CSR is the number one topic at graduate recruitment fairs and that online recruitment statistics show graduates looking for jobs also visit the pages about the bank's CSR programmes. Wright says:

> CSR is a key factor in recruitment and retention. For today's graduates it can be the deal breaker when considering companies offering roughly the same packages, as the banking sector does. Graduates want to be part of a culture and CSR is a part of that.

Customers too increasingly expect business to play its part in society, particularly in the aftermath of the banking crisis and tax-avoidance allegations. Customers are willing to vote with their feet if businesses act badly. Former chairman of Lloyds Bank, Victor Blank, wrote in a 2011 article calling for a new philanthropy for the 21st Century:

> Businesses have a strong incentive to get involved, not just because of altruism or to rehabilitate themselves after the crunch, but because customers are demanding responsible corporate citizenship.
>
> Programmes of employee engagement, where companies make time

65 | John Stone, a Beacon Award winner in 2013, founded the Stone Family Foundation with an initial endowment of £50 million in 2005.

available for their employees, combined with enhanced philanthropic giving, can make massive improvements to society and, ultimately, benefit the bottom line also. As companies look to their future in a post-credit crunch era, perhaps it is time to rewrite the old proverb and adopt the motto that Charity Begins at Work.

CITY INSTITUTIONS AND PHILANTHROPY

The City and London can boast a plethora of organisations and institutions committed to charitable giving and voluntary action. It is one of the world's philanthropic capitals. Among its greatest and oldest are the City's livery companies, effectively the first trading standards bodies, whose roots can be traced back to 1066. They have grown to become a powerhouse of philanthropy. Though companies vary hugely in size, wealth and profile, with some having long-held endowments and others relying on fund-raising, they share three missions: to promote their trades, to serve their membership and to provide charitable funds for their causes.

Today's 108 Worshipful Companies are committed to continuing these traditions and have broadened their giving to make meaningful contributions to education, health, the arts and society in general, in the City, Greater London, nationally and internationally. Almost £42 million was donated by them in 2011 to causes such as education, welfare and relief, the church, the environment and to trade, according to The City of London Corporation's survey carried out by The Mercers' Company in 2011. This is around £1 million more than was donated in 2006, the last survey undertaken. Alderman Sir Michael Bear, Lord Mayor of London for 2010-11, under whose tenure the survey was commissioned, says:

> The livery companies of the City of London represent a long tradition of commitment and philanthropy – but good that is often done by stealth. What these figures – impressive though they are – can never show is the vast impact of their work; the educational opportunities created, the vulnerable supported or the expertise and time and energy given.

The statistics show some 2,500 livery company members are actively involved in the governance and stewardship of their charities and a further 1,591 are regular volunteers. Education received the lion's share of support in 2011 attracting 51% of the total figure, with 884 members volunteering in education, 464 as school or college governors.

Reinforcing the companies' long-standing tradition of philanthropy, in 2013 The Rt. Hon. the Lord Mayor Alderman Roger Gifford announced a Livery Legacy Initiative. All new liverymen and women will from now on be asked to sign a legacy form in favour of their company's charitable interests from their eventual estate. Such legacies are in the tradition of perhaps the most famous Alderman and Lord Mayor, Dick Whittington, who left the equivalent of many millions of pounds to the Mercers' Company; an endowment that is still bearing fruit.

Like the livery companies, The City of London Corporation's 800-year-old charity, Bridge House Estates, is one of the oldest and largest institutions. Today, through its grant-making arm, the City Bridge Trust, it works by bridging and strengthening communities, granting more than £16 million a year to causes across Greater London. The Trust is working at the vanguard of the sector as a strategic, innovative and influential funder. Over the decades it has led the way on key issues such as disabled access, green issues, sustainability and now impact, collaboration and social investment. In 2012 it launched its own £20 million Social Investment Fund which aims to play a major role in establishing the market. The Fund aims to achieve a positive financial return and demonstrable social benefit. It will provide loan finance, quasi-equity and equity that provides development and risk capital to organisations working towards charitable ends or with social purpose.

The livery companies and the City Bridge Trust are two of the City's largest and oldest philanthropic institutions among many hundreds large and small. They have survived by being responsive to change while sticking to tradition and continuing to do what they do well. They are emblematic of a philanthropic City and have been a constant reminder to the City of its moral obligation to society.

INDIVIDUAL PHILANTHROPY

Individual giving is vibrant among a small community of City leaders. Those who give, often do so on a grand scale. In the last decade alone we can point to many multi-million pound donations among City grandees. Sir Vernon Ellis, who led Accenture to its £10 billion flotation in 2001, donated £5 million to the Coliseum restoration project in 2006, generating a well spring of public funding needed to complete the £18 million project. He has given more than £7 million to culture and the arts and gives much of his time to the boards of its key organisations, including ENO and The British Council, as well as nurturing new talent.

Financier John Stone founded the Stone Family Foundation in 2005 with an initial endowment of £50 million from the proceeds of the reputed £124 million sale of his wealth management company Lombard International Assurance to Friends Provident in 2004. The Foundation currently invests approximately £5 million a year supporting innovative,

66 | Harvey McGrath, financier and former Prudential Chairman, received the Judges' Special Beacon Award for City Philanthropy in 2013. The award marked his support for strategic organisations and help for people from disadvantaged backgrounds to access university education and training.

sustainable and entrepreneurial approaches around the UK and in developing countries where the focus is primarily in the WASH (Water, Sanitation and Hygiene) sector.

American-born banker John Studzinski gives millions of pounds to the arts, including a £5 million donation to Tate Modern that funded a new wing. A decade ago he established the Genesis Foundation that nurtures and develops artistic excellence.

Former investment banker Sir Thomas Hughes-Hallett is a prolific philanthropist. He supports a huge range of causes, from Community Foundations and grass roots projects to medical research and agenda-moving initiatives. In 2011 he chaired the Philanthropy Review, a sector-led inquiry into philanthropy in the UK, which in June 2012 published its 'call to action' – a list of proposals to encourage more people to give and givers to give more.

In fact, as Sir Thomas is keen to emphasise, Britain is a generous nation. The 2013 *Sunday Times Giving List*, that has collected data on the country's wealthiest givers for 25 years, reveals a 20% increase in giving, which suggests the wealthy elite are 'stepping up to the mark', it says. Like-for-like giving among the top 100 philanthropists, measured by the proportion of their total wealth given away in the past year, showed a £305 million increase, rising to £1,772 million from £1,467 million. The total amount of giving tracked from 231 people in the *Sunday Times Rich List 2013*, is also up more than 21% from £1,715 million to £2,081 million, a level beaten only once in the past 12 years.

The question of why some wealthy people are so generous when so many are not has been at the nexus of lively debate for many years. The subject has spawned a great number of studies to explore what motivates wealthy philanthropists, including the just published new edition of *Why Rich People Give* by Theresa Lloyd, a philanthropy advisor and fundraiser for many years, and Dr Beth Breeze of Kent University. Research shows that connection to a cause is paramount; upbringing and family values are also key: a sense of obligation and of giving something back is often cited, as are religious beliefs.

Sir Thomas Hughes-Hallett is from a dynasty of City philanthropists. His great uncle Ian Fairbairn, 'the father of unit trusts' founded the Esmée Fairbairn Foundation in memory of his wife, also a great philanthropist and founder of the Citizens Advice Bureau, by giving all his holdings in M&G, the company he had joined some 30 years before. In 1999 the Foundation sold the shares as part of M&G's takeover by Prudential Corporation PLC for £800 million. Sir Thomas describes it as 'a great

67 | The City Funding Network is an open-giving circle, created for young City professionals to socialise around giving. At its first two events it raised almost £50,000.

Photo courtesy of Mal Chadwick/ The Funding Network

explosion of generosity'. The Esmée Fairbairn Foundation, of which Sir Thomas is a trustee, now grants £40 million a year and is one of the world's leading independent funders.

Sir Thomas is a passionate advocate for more philanthropy and speaks openly about his giving, which he says leads people to accuse him of being 'a show off'.

> I talk about my giving because I want to encourage others to experience the joy that comes with philanthropy. The best way to encourage philanthropy is to celebrate it as a social norm. I can't emphasise enough the fun that philanthropy brings. Philanthropy is not painful. You have to get satisfaction from philanthropy and you shouldn't be embarrassed about that.

He is openly disappointed by the levels of giving among the 'professional classes' and the 'mass affluent' whom he feels have lost the sense of community that is still enjoyed by poorer neighbourhoods. Research shows that though the wealthy contribute the most in money terms, as a percentage of their income they give less than those on much smaller salaries.

Sir Thomas gives an example of the low levels of giving among the wealthy:

> I gave £50,000 to the Kensington and Chelsea Community Foundation and it was the largest gift they had ever received. I was shocked that in one of the wealthiest boroughs in the world that was their largest donation. In Manhattan it would have been £50 million.

However, the £100,000 he donated to the Suffolk Community Foundation that he also spoke about at meetings and to the press, led to more donations as he had hoped: 'I was delighted to receive a phone call from them saying I was no longer their single largest donor.'

Sir Thomas is also irked by the fact that the US has overtaken Britain in the

68 | Young Philanthropy, seen here at the 2013 Beacon Awards where the syndicate received an award. Members are pictured with Lord Mayor Roger Gifford (centre) and Martyn Lewis CBE (far left), the broadcaster and chair of the National Council of Voluntary Organisations.

giving leagues, particularly as the UK and especially the City have been so philanthropic for so long. One of the only surveys to offer a world comparison, *The World Giving Index*, published in 2011 by CAF, shows the USA in top spot, with the UK making it to fifth. A previous survey from CAF carried out in 2006 shows that while the US gives around 2% of its GDP, the UK manages just 0.73% of its GDP.

It is impossible to put figures on the City's philanthropic contribution owing to a lack of coherent data that can pinpoint donations geographically, particularly as the donors are global firms or citizens with several offices or addresses. The preferred anonymity of many donors confounds the aim further. However, the *Coutts Million Pound Donors Report 2012* that annually records single donations by individuals and institutions in excess of a million pounds has produced a London figure. The survey offers some grounds for optimism, showing a greater number of gifts (232) than the previous year. However it also revealed a lower mean average (£1.2 million) equating to a total of £1.24 billion. Donors based in London now account for well over half (62%) of all donations worth £1 million or more, up from 56% in 2009/10. Taken with many other surveys it confirms London as the epicentre of the UK's charitable giving among its wealthiest individuals. And it points to the City as a flag bearer for philanthropy as *The Give and Let Give* report highlighted.

CITY PHILANTHROPY'S NEXT GENERATION

There are strong indications that a new generation of City professionals, the 'Square Mile millennials', will move the needle on giving in the City. Indeed, the three-year campaign City Philanthropy – A Wealth of Opportunity (for which I declare an interest as its development manager), is aimed at embedding philanthropy in the careers of all young City professionals. In 2012 the initiative launched The City Funding Network, an open giving circle for young professionals. Organised by The Funding Network (TFN), that pioneered open-giving circles in the UK a decade ago, and funded by City of London Corporation's charity, City Bridge Trust, the network brings like-minded young people together to socialise around philanthropy, widen their networks and meet inspiring charities. Its first two lively meetings raised almost £50,000 for six niche charities, who pitched Dragon's Den style to the 60 plus assembled young philanthropists. TFN co-founder Dr Frederick Mulder CBE says the idea is to put 'the fun in funding'.

Other similar giving networks for young professionals of both sexes, have also sprung up over the last few years and point to a new appetite for ethics, social responsibility and philanthropy in the City. In early 2011, the Young Philanthropy Syndicate (YPS) launched with the aim of encouraging young professionals into philanthropy. The model enables groups to join together and invest their money, time and skills in a niche charity project, with matched funding and the support of an experienced philanthropist and their employer.

Sixteen syndicates are now up and running, investing approximately £96,000 over 12 months in a range of projects. There are 24 more syndicates due to launch in 2013 and will invest approximately £144,000. YPS has established a strong pipeline of new syndicates at existing employers, including PwC, Deloitte, KPMG, E&Y and the Civil Service with plans to pilot syndicates across a number of City firms in the coming months.

Adam Pike, YPS co-founder, who is taking a sabbatical from audit tax and consulting firm Deloitte to build the network, says he and fellow-founder Mike Harris were inspired by Bill and Melinda Gates' and Warren Buffett's Giving Pledge. It invites billionaires to give away the majority of their wealth to good causes. In 2013 it had 114 signatories from around the world including Britons Richard Branson and Lord Ashcroft. Pike explains:

> At the time, we had both just made the transition from youth work to jobs in the City. As recent graduates, we had limited resources but wanted to continue to contribute in a meaningful way and impact on the causes we cared about. We spoke with friends and colleagues and were not surprised to hear of their passion on many issues with ideas to match. However, we lacked the means and platform to influence and create a positive lasting impact. It became clear that as a group we possessed significant collective wealth, energy and experience that had not been mobilised by existing funding models. We see each new Young Philanthropy Syndicate as a Giving Pledge in its own right; a commitment to invest in a niche initiative that will transform people's lives.

69 | The Bread Tin is a giving club for young professionals, who create their own charitable projects with the support of a matching donor.

In the same year as the launch of YPS, a group of Oxford University students started the 80,000 Hours campaign (referencing the average amount of hours we work in a life time) to encourage young people to give 10% of their time or money to good causes during the length of their working careers. The campaign also encourages young people to choose high-impact ethical careers that will enhance their ability to further good causes. Founder Will Crouch, a DPhil student in ethics, suggests controversially that becoming a high-earning banker with a social conscience is more impactful than being a poorly paid aid worker:

> Everyone knows that when you go into a high-earning career you can earn absurdly large amounts of money. An average banker might earn about £6 million over a 30-year career. When we see that number we get just as angry about bankers' bonuses as anyone else, but we also see an opportunity. Say you decided to donate about half of that. You'd still be immensely well-off. But you would also be giving a lot: enough to employ several doctors in the developing world, or even to set up a charity to do almost anything you like!

It's not a view that has been wholly accepted but it is one that challenges the status quo.

Other networks such as The Bread Tin and the Engaging Experience Philanthropy Network that have been established in the last few years are offering a range of opportunities for young City professionals to socialise around philanthropy, raise hundreds of thousands of pounds for niche charitable projects as well as donate their skills and knowledge. Peter West, Bread Tin founder, says:

> The vision is to create a new generation of philanthropists; to transform the attitudes and circumstances of the youngest strata of graduates, young professionals and wealthy individuals in The City of London today; to address a culture of apathy and individualistic consumerism and to encourage a widespread trend among young professionals towards idealism and a growing ethical conscience.

By lowering the access point for taking part – for the price of a daily coffee these young people are engaging in strategic, impactful charitable giving – these networks are democratising philanthropy and putting it in the reach of early career City professionals who have yet to make their fortunes. The hope is by the time they have acquired wealth, they will also have acquired the knowledge, skills and networks, as fully-fledged philanthropists, to put it to good use.

LOOKING AHEAD

This chapter has given just a few examples of the City's philanthropy among its various constituencies. It paints a picture of vibrant, innovative and entrepreneurial philanthropic communities. It reveals a style of giving characteristic of the City – risk-taking, reward-seeking and result-producing. We see a 'macro' approach, hand-ups rather than hand-outs, and a preference to look at the bigger picture and deal with cause rather than symptoms with a wish to bring transformational and systemic change. City philanthropists are active and engaged and want to enjoy the benefits that philanthropy brings when one can make a difference.

While giving levels are stubbornly low, for example as a percentage of GDP, many of the surveys cited show pockets of extreme generosity. These examples give grounds for optimism. And while we can look back to a long history of philanthropy we can also look forward to a new generation of philanthropists who are bringing youthful enthusiasm, new energy and creativity to giving. With a show of leadership from City elders and a strong political and economic wind behind them, it's just possible the scene is set for the Square Mile to return to its roots as a philanthropy powerhouse – not as a 'white-washing' exercise but because it makes business sense for those companies promoting it and those individuals involved.

As former Lloyds chairman Victor Blank said in a recent *Daily Telegraph* article:
> Philanthropy on its own will not – and should not – restore the damage to the reputation of banks or rebuild their moral capital: the scale of that task should not be underestimated. But, along with commitment to best business values, it has a part to play for companies wanting to regain the trust and respect of communities in which they operate.

The exhibition *Philanthropy: The City Story* that this book accompanies is a celebration of the achievements of philanthropy through the ages. The City Philanthropy – Wealth of Opportunity initiative will continue its work helping to embed philanthropy as part of a professional career in the City and support London and the UK in reclaiming its position at the top of the world giving league.

GLOSSARY

As philanthropy evolves and moves into new spheres, such as the world of investment, so its language expands. Terms are not always agreed and much work is being done on creating a common language for social investment by the Global Impact Investing Network (GIIN). This listing references the source of definitions' to 'This listing offers a range of current definitions, with sources referenced.

Impact investing (also Social investment): Impact investments are investments made into companies, organizations, and funds with the intention to generate measurable social and environmental impact alongside a financial return. They can be made in both emerging and developed markets, and target a range of returns from below market to market rate, depending upon the circumstances. **(Definition: Global Impact Investing Network)**

Micro-finance: Micro-finance is a general term to describe financial services to low-income individuals or to those who do not have access to typical banking services. **(Definition: Kiva)**

Philanthrocapitalism: A phrase coined by Matthew Bishop, US Business Editor and New York Bureau Chief of *The Economist*, and economist Michael Green that describes how business concepts and investment principles are being applied to philanthropy in the search for greater impact and measurable results. **(Definition: City Philanthropy – A Wealth of Opportunity)**

Philanthropy: The giving or investing of resources in an engaged and strategic way for maximum social impact and in a tax efficient manner. Resources include money, assets, time, talent, voice and social capital. **(Definition: City Philanthropy – A Wealth of Opportunity)**

Social enterprise: A social enterprise is a business with primarily social objectives whose surpluses are principally reinvested for that purpose in the business or in the community, rather than being driven by the need to maximise profit for shareholders and owners. **(Definition: DTI, 2002)**

Social Impact: Social impact is generally understood as the difference an organisation or project makes to the social problem it seeks to solve. It is the progress made towards achieving a goal—whether that is to reduce homelessness, eradicate malaria or improve educational attainment. **(Definition: New Philanthropy Capital)**

Social investment (also Impact investment): Social investment is the provision of repayable finance to charities and other social enterprises with the aim of creating social impact, and sometimes generating a financial return. It is also known as impact investing or social finance. **(Definition: New Philanthropy Capital)**

Venture philanthropy: An active approach to philanthropy, which involves giving skills as well as money. It uses the principles of venture capital, with the investee organisation receiving management support, specialist expertise and financial resources. The emphasis is on a social, rather than financial, return. **(Definition: Impetus Trust)**

FURTHER READING

Give and Let Give – Building a Culture of Philanthropy in the Financial Services Industry, 2007 published by The Policy Exchange.

Philanthrocapitalism: How Giving Can Save The World, 2010, published by A & C Black Publishers.

Grantmaking by UK Trusts and Charities, 2007, published by CAF. http://www.acf.org.uk/uploadedFiles/Publications_and_resources/Publications /0416B_TrustAndFoundationBriefingPaper.pdf

UK Giving, published by NCVO and CAF. https://www.cafonline.org/publications/2012-publications/uk-giving-2012.aspx

Virtuous Capital: What Foundations Can Learn From Venture Capital,1997, published by Harvard Business Review. http://www.wheatridge.org/wp-content/uploads/2012/03/Virtuous_Capital_HB.pdf

Venture Philanthropy in the UK, 2011, published by Factary. www.factary.com .

Contributing to Communities, 2013, published by the Alternative Investment Management Association (AIMA). http://www.aima.org/en/document-summary/index.cfm/docid/183E2158-EF2F-4A25-B56792ACE84B99E8

The Company Giving Almanac, July 2013, published by Directory of Social Change (DSC).

A new philanthropy for the 21st Century, by Victor Blank, January 22 2011, published by *The Daily Telegraph*.

Livery Company Profile, 2011, published by The Mercers' Company. http://www.mercers.co.uk/sites/default/files/pictures/LiveryProfile2011%20%2 82%29.pdf

The Investor Perspectives on Social Enterprise Financing, July 2011, published by the City of London Corporation. http://www.cityoflondon.gov.uk/business/economic-research-and-information/research-publications/Pages/investor-perspectives-on-social-enterprise-financing.aspx

Why Rich People Give, 2013 by Theresa Lloyd and Dr Beth Breeze.

The Coutts Million Pound Donors report, 2012, Dr Beth Breeze, published by Coutts in Association with the Centre for Philanthropy at the University of Kent. http://www.kent.ac.uk/sspssr/cphsj/documents/Million-Pound-Donor-Report-2012.pdf

World Giving Index, 2011, published by CAF. https://www.cafonline.org/pdf/world_giving_index_2011_191211.pdf

USEFUL ORGANISATIONS

100 Women in Hedge Funds (100WHF): www.100womeninhedgefunds.org

80,000 Hours: www.80000hours.org

ARK (Absolute Return for Kids): www.ark.co.uk

Association of Charitable Foundations (ACF): www.acf.org.uk

Charities Evaluation Services (CES): www.ces-vol.org.uk

CIFF (Children's Investment Fund Foundation): www.ciff.org

City Bridge Trust (CBT): www.citybridgetrust.org.uk

Directory for Social Change (DSC): www.dsc.org.uk

Dragon Awards: www.dragonawards.org.uk

Engaging Experience Philanthropy Network: www.bulldogtrust.org/philanthropy_network.htm

Esmée Fairbairn Foundation: www.esmeefairbairn.org.uk

European Venture Philanthropy Association (EVPA): www.evpa.eu.com

Heart of the City (HoTC): www.theheartofthecity.com

Hedge Funds Care: www.hedgefundscare.org

Impetus-The Private Equity Foundation: www.impetus-pef.org.uk

John Stone Family Foundation: www.thesff.com

New Philanthropy Capital (NPC): www.thinknpc.org

Pilotlight: www.pilotlight.org.uk

The Bread Tin: www.thebreadtin.org

The City Funding Network: www.thefundingnetwork.org.uk/city-funding-network

The Philanthropy Review: www.philanthropyreview.co.uk

Young Philanthropy: www.youngphilanthropy.org.uk

'MONEY IS LIKE WATER, IT IS A GREAT THING. WE ALL NEED IT IN ORDER TO LIVE... WHEN IT TURNS INTO A TSUNAMI AND WE DROWN IN IT, OBVIOUSLY IT BECOMES A VERY BAD THING'

Ronald Cohen, 2013